HARROW

The Story of a Millennium

Don Walter

Harrow, Kenton, Pinner, Roxeth, Stanmore, Wealdstone

Published with the financial assistance of the Advisory Panel for Local History Publications

This one is for
Emily Olivia Modaresi
and
George Robert Gorrod
children of the New Millennium

Cover illustration © Edmond Terakopian 1999
Production and design: Nikki Easton and Tracey Bohane

ISBN 1 900 306 13 1
Published by Orpheus Publications Limited
7 St John's Road, Harrow, Middlesex HA1 2EE
Tel: 020 8863 2020 Fax: 020 8863 2444
www.orpheuspublications.com

Printed and bound in Great Britain by BAS Printers Limited.

Author's note

A thousand ages in thy sight
Are like an evening gone;
Short as the watch that ends the night
Before the rising sun.

I Watts (Hymns Ancient & Modern)

I am all too aware that a 1000-year-history of Harrow, touching, however briefly, on just about every district of our present borough, could have been very long – and, dare one say it, very dull.

An early decision was therefore made to keep this volume reasonably short and to keep firmly in mind the interests of the general reader who wishes to be entertained as well as informed.

For such reasons, I have had to be both highly selective in my choice of material and extremely concise in its presentation. This is especially true of the chapters dealing with our present century, which are largely my own interpretation of our recent past.

If, however, my book stimulates an appetite for greater detail – and this is very much my hope – readers are reminded that the Bibliography at its close lists many titles which should interest them as much as they have assisted me.

On the theme of assistance, I must also record my especial gratitude to Bob Mills, our Library Services Manager and the Advisory Panel for Local History Publications (chaired by forme councillor Owen Cock) for their agreement to assist the project financially through an income share agreement. Bob Thomson, our Local History Librarian, not only gave me unfettered access to the Harrow Local History Collection but also agreed to read the text – not once but twice! Sheena Crawley, Editor of the Harrow Observer, and her photographic team, have also been notably helpful in the provision of invaluable material, including much from the paper's archives.

Finally, I am delighted to record that the publishers of this book are the very local and very dedicated Orpheus Publications Ltd who, I am confident, will here exceed their much-admired presentation of my earlier "A Lookback At Harrow".

Don Walter
Harrow on the Hill
September 1999

Foreword

I know I will join many others in welcoming Don Walter's account of the last thousand years of life in Harrow. As would be expected from his previous publications he has provided us with an entertaining and readable account of the history of the borough with its ups and downs across the centuries.

This book is the product of a partnership between a local author, a local newspaper, the borough's local history library, an advisory panel of Councillors and representatives of local history interests, and a local publisher. I believe the partnership has given us a book to enhance our pride in our borough.

I look forward to the new Harrow Partnership (end Chapter 42) further enhancing the life of the borough and leading us to new ventures for future historians to record in the new millennium.

The Worshipful the Mayor
Councillor Ann Groves
Mayor's Parlour
Civic Centre
London Borough of Harrow
September 1999

I am delighted to welcome the first local history book to attempt the difficult task of telling over a thousand years of the Harrow story.

I first became fascinated by Harrow's history as a school pupil and have relished the opportunity Don Walter provides to delve further into Harrow's rich and fascinating history.

This book has been made possible by the collaboration of many different people in the borough who rightly see its publication as a matter of some civic pride. In particular thanks are due to Bob Mills, Harrow's Library Services Manager, the Local History Publication Panel for their kind funding, as well as the Civic Centre Library and the Harrow Observer which have been generous in sharing invaluable items from their archives.

Gareth Thomas MP
Westminster
September 1999

Contents

The Church receives the Harrow lands – one of nine clerestory windows at St. Mary's inspired by events in history.

1. Harrow at Domesday

In the great span of Time, one thousand years is no time at all so it is no surprise that, around the year AD 1000, several places within the present Borough of Harrow already had sizeable communities with a clearly defined social structure.

The source of our knowledge is that most detailed and authoritative of all historical records, the *Domesday Book*, compiled about 1086 by the conquering William I of Normandy in an attempt to establish the extent of the land he had wrested from King Harold at the Battle of Hastings some 20 years before.

William almost certainly knew this record as *The Book of The Treasury* but, in successive centuries, a suitably awe-struck populace thought it more appropriate to use a name (Doomsday or Domesday) clearly evoking the Biblical Day of Judgement, when all things shall be accounted.

Though the Harrow entry, under the name of Herges, is only one of many manors, it must have had a special significance for King William as the Lordship of the Harrow Manor then belonged to Archbishop Lanfranc, who was not only the King's Archbishop of Canterbury, but also his close personal friend.

In the circumstances, one might be forgiven for thinking that a conqueror had simply decided to share some of his spoils but, in fact, Canterbury's hold on Harrow was an historic one, dating back to a well-documented exchange of lands between Crown and Church in the year AD 825. Lanfranc was, therefore, only one of a number of archbishops to hold the Harrow Manor over a period of centuries.

The Harrow Manor was a sizeable one, assessed in Domesday at 100 hides (which equates to some 12,000 ploughable acres). This, moreover, makes no acknowledgement of wasteland which Domesday consistently excludes from its reckonings.

At the Manor's heart, there would almost certainly have been some sort of Manor House, most probably on the same hilltop site that in the 13th century became the Rectory Manor.

Whether there was also a church on the Hill is not recorded since the great record book was more concerned with land, which is permanent, than with buildings, which are inevitably temporary: nevertheless, several strong pieces of evidence point us to this conclusion.

The first is Domesday's reference to a priest at Harrow and, what's more, one in possession of a whole hide of land.

The second is Lanfranc's decision, even while Domesday was in the course of compilation, to found a church on Harrow Hill in the name of St. Mary.

This could, of course, have been a brand-new church. But, equally plausibly, it could well have been a more impressive replacement for some small Saxon edifice that an earlier

Archbishop Lanfranc – as portrayed in a Victorian stained glass window in the tower of St. Mary's.

archbishop had placed there; after all, at Domesday the Church had already owned the land for over 160 years.

As the Domesday Book records, Harrow's priest was, in fact, only one of at least 117 people then living on the Harrow Manor.

To appreciate just who they were – and the roles they then fulfilled – it may be useful to recall a few details of the administrative structure that the Norman King William had inherited from his Saxon predecessors.

As a shire (or county), Middlesex was divided into regions known as Hundreds, of which what is now the Borough of Harrow occupied the Hundred of Gore – a term which, as many will recall, survived as a Petty Sessional district until comparatively recent times.

For convenience, the Hundreds were further sub-divided into "vills" from which the word "village" springs and "tuns", a forerunner of our present "towns".

As for a manor, this normally consisted of two parts. There was the demesne, which the Lord retained for his own support and the villeinage, which was parcelled out among the villeins and the cottagers who gave service to the Lord as required. In addition to these bondsmen, there were also the serfs whom we would now regards as slaves.

Harrow at Domesday was in no way atypical. Apart from the priest, there were three knights, seven vassals (the knight's tenants), 102 villeins, two cottagers and two serfs, making a total of 117 persons; however, since it is usually accepted that only the heads of households were listed, this number can easily be trebled, or even quadrupled, giving us a community of some size and importance.

This view is confirmed by Domesday's many analysts who have calculated that the Harrow listing was not only the biggest in the county but the third most valuable.

Although the entry for Herges rightly takes precedence in our narrative, it is no less worthy of record that Great Stanmore (Stanmore Magna) also earns a place in Domesday, where it is recorded as Stanmere. This conflation of the Old English "stan" and "mere", meaning a stony mere or pool, had earlier appeared in a document of AD 793, in which King Offa of Mercia and his sons granted ten "mansiones" (holdings) in Stanmere as part of the foundation of St. Alban's Abbey.

By the time of Domesday, however, nine and a half hides of land were held by Robert, Count of Mortain, who was William The Conqueror's half-brother, although this land was later restored to the Church.

As with Herges, a priest is listed, suggesting that Great Stanmore, too, had its own Saxon church.

In addition, a further nine and a half hides at Little Stanmore (Stanmore Parva, or, later still, Whitchurch) can be found under "The land of Roger de Raismes". Similarly, the present-day Kingsbury makes two appearances: one under the Abbot of St. Peter's, Westminster the other, under the landowner, Ernulf de Hesden.

For the most part, of course, we can only guess at the details of their life-style, nevertheless it is fascinating to realise that, a full thousand years ago, people not so very different from ourselves were already working the land, raising their families and enjoying worship where today's infinitely larger and more varied population still works and plays and occasionally prays.

In *HVND* de Gara . tenet . L . archieps *HERGES*.
Pro . c . hid ſe defendeb T.R.E. 7 m facit. Tra . ē . LXX.
car. Ad dniu ptin . XXX . hide . 7 ibi ſunt . IIII . carucæ.
7 v . pot fieri . Int franc 7 uilt . XLV . car . 7 XVI.
plus poſs . ee . Ibi pbr . I . hidā . 7 III . milites . VI . hid
7 ſub eis manent . VII . hōes . Ibi . XIII . uilti qſq; dim
hid . 7 XXVIII . uilti qſq; de . I . uirg . 7 XLVIII . uilt
qſq; dim uirg . 7 XIII . uilt de . IIII . hid . 7 II . cot de
XIII . acris . 7 II . ſerui . Paſta ad pecun uillæ . Silua
II . mil porc . In totis ualentijs ual . LVI . lib.
7 qdo recep . XX . lib . T.R.E. LX . lib . Hoc Maner
ten Leuuin com die qua rex . E . fuit uiuus 7 mortuus.

The entry for Harrow (Herges) as it appears in the Domesday Book, AD 1086.

2. The Consecration of St. Mary's

Within a few short years of the appearance of the Domesday Book there occurred the first truly momentous event in the history of Harrow.

This was the consecration of the parish church of St. Mary's, Harrow on the Hill, in January 1094.

By then, the realm had both a new king and a new archbishop and both men were very different personalities from their predecessors.

In particular, William I had been succeeded - without dispute, it has to be admitted - by his son, variously known as William Rufus or William The Red. A young man, only 27 at his coronation, he seems to have been both weak and avaricious. He also surrounded himself with unsuitable and unscrupulous companions such as Ranulf Flambard, whose family were to become increasingly well known in Harrow.

It appears to have been Flambard who first conceived an audaciously simple way of diverting money from the Church to the Crown. Whenever an important ecclesiastical post became vacant, no new incumbent was sought; instead, the relevant income was appropriated for the King.

Even Canterbury itself was not sacrosanct and, a full four years after the death of Archbishop Lanfranc in 1096, a new appointment was still awaited.

William Rufus now fell ill and, in a notably superstitious era, came to believe his illness was a sign of God's displeasure. By the same token, he seems to have convinced himself that the appointment of a new archbishop might bring about a recovery.

In reality, there was only one serious candidate - Anselm who had succeeded Lanfranc as Prior of the great monastic house of Bec in Normandy. If we are to believe Anselm's chronicler, generally known as "the Good Monk" Eadmer (who admittedly seized every opportunity to denigrate William Rufus), Anselm was all but forced into accepting the Primacy; indeed, on discovering the true nature of the monarch, Anselm was later to describe himself as "an old and feeble sheep yoked to an untameable bull".

Such details have particular relevance to our Harrow story for they may very well explain why a full seven years separated the foundation of St. Mary's and its actual consecration.

Of course, given the difficulties of transporting materials to the church's hill-top site, the purely physical act of building might have occupied every single moment from 1087 to 1094. Alternatively – and it seems an entirely plausible theory – St. Mary's might possibly have been completed much earlier than 1094 and then remained without consecration until such time as William Rufus saw fit to appoint an Archbishop.

Further credence to this view may be provided by the fact that only a single month separates Anselm's own consecration as Primate from his consecration of St. Mary's.

Portrait of Archbishop Anselm, later canonised as St. Anselm.

The consecration ceremony – as depicted in stained glass at St. Mary's.

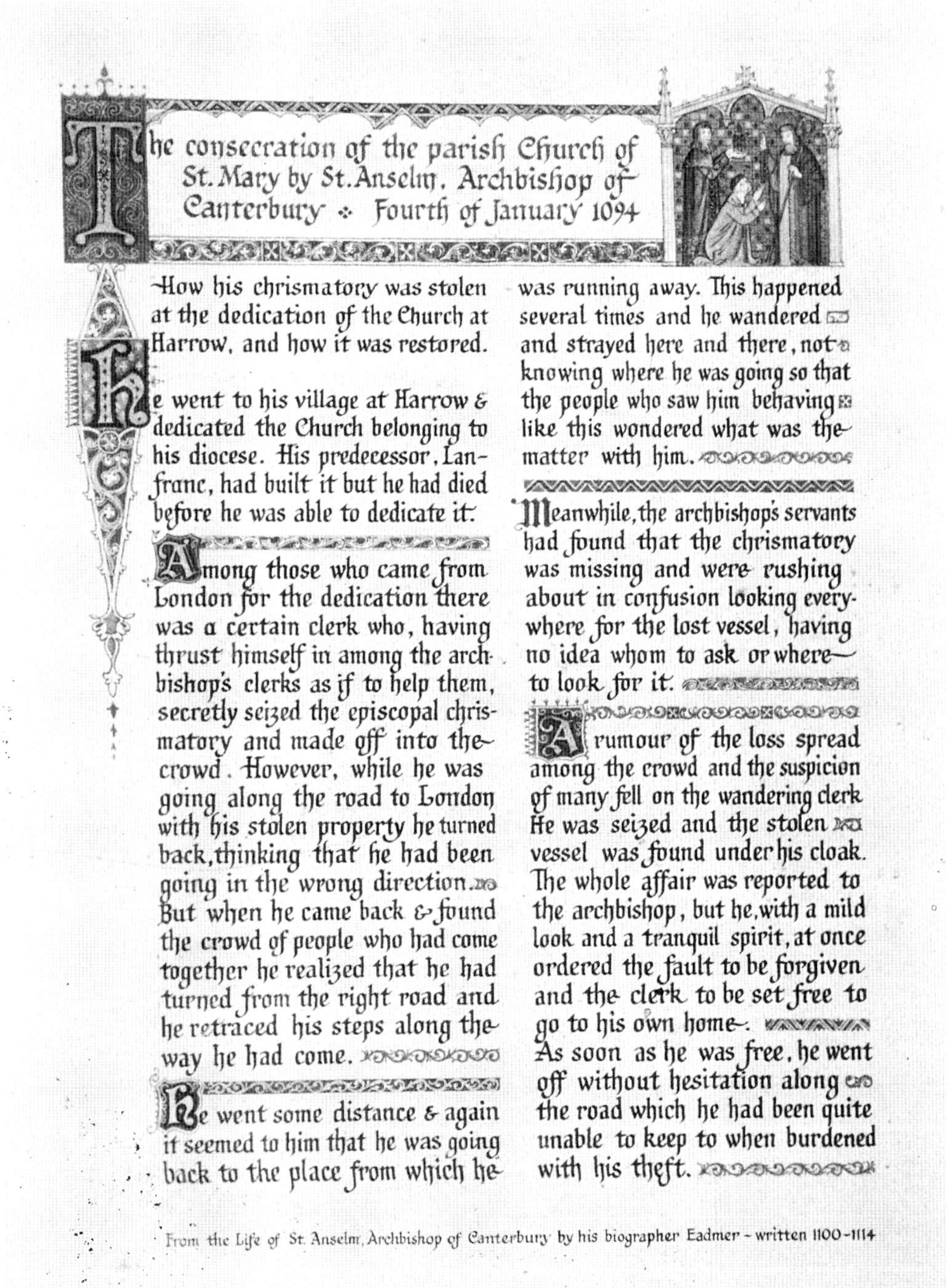

The consecration of the parish Church of St. Mary by St. Anselm, Archbishop of Canterbury ∴ Fourth of January 1094

How his chrismatory was stolen at the dedication of the Church at Harrow, and how it was restored.

He went to his village at Harrow & dedicated the Church belonging to his diocese. His predecessor, Lanfranc, had built it but he had died before he was able to dedicate it.

Among those who came from London for the dedication there was a certain clerk who, having thrust himself in among the archbishop's clerks as if to help them, secretly seized the episcopal chrismatory and made off into the crowd. However, while he was going along the road to London with his stolen property he turned back, thinking that he had been going in the wrong direction. But when he came back & found the crowd of people who had come together he realized that he had turned from the right road and he retraced his steps along the way he had come.

He went some distance & again it seemed to him that he was going back to the place from which he was running away. This happened several times and he wandered and strayed here and there, not knowing where he was going so that the people who saw him behaving like this wondered what was the matter with him.

Meanwhile, the archbishop's servants had found that the chrismatory was missing and were rushing about in confusion looking everywhere for the lost vessel, having no idea whom to ask or where to look for it.

A rumour of the loss spread among the crowd and the suspicion of many fell on the wandering clerk. He was seized and the stolen vessel was found under his cloak. The whole affair was reported to the archbishop, but he, with a mild look and a tranquil spirit, at once ordered the fault to be forgiven and the clerk to be set free to go to his own home. As soon as he was free, he went off without hesitation along the road which he had been quite unable to keep to when burdened with his theft.

From the Life of St. Anselm, Archbishop of Canterbury by his biographer Eadmer – written 1100–1114

Eadmer's account of the troubled consecration.

Given this troubled background, it would be nice to think that the consecration ceremony itself passed without incident - but Eadmer has a very different story to tell.

It seems that Maurice, then Bishop of London, felt the consecration was rightfully his to perform. To his credit, Anselm had the good sense to refer the question to the 85-year-old Wulfstan, the one surviving Saxon bishop and a revered elder statesman of the Church. Unsurprisingly perhaps, Wulfstan ruled in favour of the more senior cleric. But that was far from the end of the matter.

According to Eadmer, the Bishop of London's reaction was an attempt to sabotage the consecration ceremony. The story goes that a clerk in his service smuggled himself into the company of the Archbishop's clerks and then made off with the episcopal chrismatory, a key vessel in the conduct of the service.

It would seem that the thief was apprehended in the nick of time, although Eadmer has his own version of events in which he describes how the thief, unable to find his way off the Hill, keeps returning to this starting point and thus arouses suspicion.

The full story with its quasi-miraculous embellishments makes fascinating reading. Happily, visitors to St. Mary's can still read a printed version which is permanently on display just inside the church's main south door.

Flambards, the 18th century house in Harrow Hill's High Street which takes its name from the once-influential Flambard family.

A rare portrait of Thomas Becket, Archbishop, Chancellor and Martyr.

3. Becket and Harrow

As we move into the twelfth century, Harrow's traditional link with Canterbury provides our story with one of its most colourful characters – Thomas Becket, the Archbishop whose troubled friendship with his King, Henry II, ultimately brought about his own murder.

It is to the credit of contemporary chroniclers, such as William FitzStephen, that far more is known about Thomas Becket than would seem possible for a life lived over 800 years ago.

We know, for example, that he was the son of a one-time Sheriff of London who had once been a neighbour in Normandy of the distinguished churchman Theobald.

We know, too, that the ambitious young Thomas, realising that his quickest route of advancement lay within the Church, persuaded his father to effect an introduction to Theobald, now Archbishop of Canterbury – and, of course, Lord of the Manor of Harrow.

It was, therefore "at the town of Harrow", that Thomas Becket ultimately joined the Archbishop's court.

In recording the early years of Becket's career, FitzStephen also relates one of those near-miraculous anecdotes that are not infrequently found in the lives of those destined for sainthood.

Yet even if apocryphal, the story deserves retelling here for it directly concerns our Harrow parish church.

It seems that Becket, together with his travelling companion, one Ralph Baille-Hache, spent his first night at Harrow lodging at an inn, possibly some predecessor of the much later King's Head Hotel.

That night, the hostess of the inn had a dream in which she claimed to see one of her two visitors seated on the roof of St. Mary's in such a way that his robes seemed to cover the entire edifice. As FitzStephen relates the story, "On the morrow she told her husband of her dream and put upon it the interpretation that one of the young men (for as yet she knew not whither of the two was Thomas) would hereafter be ruler of the church pertaining to the Manor."

In fact, Thomas Becket's assumption of the Primacy occurred even more quickly than she might have dreamed. The astute Theobald, faced with a new and young King (the 21-year-old Henry II), felt that it would be politic to have a loyal and relatively youthful churchman close to the throne. Thus Thomas, already a deacon of Canterbury, found himself translated from the Archbishop's court to that of the King.

In the event, the ploy worked so well that king and churchman became the closest of friends and Henry subsequently made Thomas Becket his Chancellor. Then, when Theobald himself died, Henry had Thomas consecrated as the new Archbishop of Canterbury.

Though undoubtedly intended to bring them even closer, the King's action merely served

Within ten years of Becket's death, St. Mary's had acquired its beautiful marble font.

Little remains of the St. Mary's Becket knew except for the Norman arch above the age-old west door, seen here in an engraving of 1810.

to reveal the first fatal cracks in their friendship.

Thomas insisted on resigning the Chancellorship, which was totally contrary to the King's wishes. Furthermore, as Archbishop, he quickly left no doubt that the dictates of God would always come before the commands of a mere man, even if that man happened to wear a crown.

Their first serious clash concerned the so-called clerical immunity whereby those in holy orders could be tried by their peers even for the most serious of crimes.

Concerned by earlier scandals in which guilty clerics had either received ludicrously light sentences or totally escaped punishment, the King desired that any priest convicted of a major crime be delivered up to the officers of the royal court to be dealt with according to the laws of the land.

At a great Council of Westminster in 1163, the King would undoubtedly have gained the bishops' assent but for the vehemence with which Becket argued the contrary view.

Becket now returned to his Manor at Harrow to await emissaries from Pope Alexander III whose support he had sought in the matter. The Pope did, indeed, send three papal messengers to Harrow. But the message was not the one Becket wished to hear because, for his own good reasons, the Pope had no wish to offend the King of England.

On the further deterioration of their relationship, Becket felt it advisable to flee the King's realm and appeal in person to the Pope. By then, however, the Pope was in exile in France, the Vatican having been invaded by the Emperor Frederick I (known as Barbarossa).

Then, in 1170, Henry greatly harmed his cause by having the Archbishop of York crown his elder son, Young Henry. Although this attempt to protect the succession had many precedents, it further angered Becket who, in happier times, had taken charge of the boy's education. It also infuriated the French king, Louis, because the ceremony was performed without the participation of his daughter, Margaret, who many years before had been betrothed to Young Henry; indeed, Becket himself had negotiated the alliance.

The Pope was equally incensed and, fearing that all had turned against him, King Henry agreed to meet Becket on French soil. On the surface, the reconciliation was a total success, Becket even agreeing to return to England, but the choleric temperament of both men soon thwarted their best intentions.

The King elected to remain in France and Becket was obliged to return alone with his retinue but not before he had dispatched letters suspending the Archbishop of York for his part in the coronation ceremony.

If anything, Becket's homecoming proved too great a triumph and his enemies reported to the Young King that he was "careering about the Kingdom at the head of a strong force of armed men". Later, while en route to Woodstock in Oxfordshire to pay his respects to the Young King, Becket was halted at Southwark and instructed to return to Canterbury.

Instead Becket travelled to Harrow, arriving on or about St. Lucy Day, Sunday the thirteenth of December, 1170.

Though we can never be entirely sure of his motives, the choice of Harrow made sense for many reasons. It was relatively close to Southwark, where he had been stopped and within easy access of Woodstock if the Young King were to undergo a change of heart about Becket's proposed visit.

He may even have had what we would now call a "hidden agenda" for, since 1163, the Rector of Harrow had been Nigel de Sackville, often referred to as "the usurping Rector", since his appointment had been made by the King in Becket's absence.

In the circumstances, it would be hardly surprising if Becket did not seize an opportunity to reassert his full authority in a place which undoubtedly held a special significance for him. Moreover, Becket also wished to consult with his loyal friend, Abbot Simon of St. Alban's Abbey.

From the later writings of Matthew Paris, who was chief copyist at the Abbey, we know that Abbot Simon not only came to Harrow but also offered to travel to Woodstock to intercede for Becket at the Young King's court.

Matthew Paris leaves us in no doubt of the hostility of Abbot Simon's reception at Woodstock. "There were some who clenched their fists", he writes, "and others who half drew their knives, all swearing horribly that but for a very little barrier hindered them from disembowelling or even worse the messenger who came from so pronounced a traitor".

With Christmas only days away, Becket announced that he would now return to Canterbury and keep "in the Church entrusted to my care such Festival as God may there provide". Even the celebration of Christmas, however, could not calm his hurt and anger. As another contemporary writer, Ralph de Diceto tells us, on Christmas Day itself Becket used his pulpit to publicly excommunicate both Nigel de Sackville and another old enemy, Robert de Broc.

Meanwhile the King, still in France, was being assured by the Archbishop of York and other churchmen (who had presumably crossed the Channel in search of revenge), that "while Thomas lives, you will have neither peace nor quiet nor see good days".

Nobody knows the King's precise response and that famous phrase – "Who will rid me of this turbulent priest?" – is almost certainly a latter-day invention, but it appears to have been violent enough for four knights of the royal household, Robert de Broc among them, to see it as a call to murder. The four subsequently met at de Broc's castle at Saltwood, near Hythe, where with a small armed force (de Broc among them), they stormed into Canterbury on Tuesday, December 29th and then into the Cathedral itself.

Some attempt seems to have been made to get Becket to utter words of submission but, steadfast in his beliefs to the very end, he submitted instead to four fatal blows delivered by massive swords.

Becket's reputation now soared in the Christian world, as assuredly as Henry's diminished; nevertheless, after much negotiation, the King was able to escape excommunication by swearing an oath exculpating himself from any complicity in the murder.

Four years later, Henry made public penance at the tomb of his erstwhile friend whom the Christian world has since canonised as St. Thomas of Canterbury.

4. The Conflict that Closed the Churches

In the latter part of the 12th century and the beginning of the 13th, England was scarcely fortunate in its choice of monarchs. The impetuous Henry II was succeeded, first by his second son, Richard I and, on the latter's death, by his youngest son John.

Richard, for all his popular lion-hearted image, consistently put his pursuit of the Crusades above all other duties required of him and spent only months in England during his 10-year reign. As for John, his quarrels with the Pope of the day, Innocent III, were to have serious consequences for his subjects, not least the people of Harrow.

The trouble all began with the death of Archbishop Hubert Walter in 1205 whereupon the monks of Canterbury not only made their own choice of a successor but, somewhat precipitately, despatched their candidate to Rome to obtain the symbols of his office.

John, however, had his own candidate for the role – needless to say, a personal friend – and angrily appealed to the Pope. Despite (or perhaps because of) John's intervention, the Pope promptly elected his own choice, Stephen Langton, then lecturing in theology at the Curia in Rome.

In retaliation, a furious John refused to allow Langton to set foot in England with the effect that, once again, the land had an Archbishop of Canterbury obliged to remain in exile.

Three years of stalemate followed after which the Pope played what he undoubtedly saw as his trump card. He solemnly placed England under an Interdict, which meant that the whole land was to be regarded as abhorrent and forsaken of God.

In practical terms, this meant the virtual closure of all churches, a considerable blow to the ordinary man since any community life at that time revolved around the nearest place of worship.

In Harrow, the hardship may have been even greater for there is evidence to suggest that St. Mary's was then in a process of rebuilding; certainly, many experts including Samuel Gardner, author of a much admired *Architectural History of the Church*, believe there was a long delay between the start of the rebuilding work and its completion.

Gardner suggests that problems of settlement might have caused a halt in the rebuilding until larger stones and more skilled workmen could be found. But the Papal Interdict, which lasted some four years, seems even more likely to have been a major factor in the delay.

Were there other establishments in the district that suffered under the Interdict?

The question is difficult to answer with any degree of assurance although Walter Druett, in his *Stanmore Through The Ages*, refers to late 19th-century evidence of a church in Great Stanmore from around 1100; also, a second church, dedicated to St. Lawrence in Little Stanmore, at much the same period.

The former almost certainly stood on the site of the first recorded Great Stanmore parish church which was built in the early 1300s at the junction of what became Old Church Lane

Headstone Manor, seen as a working farm earlier this century, was home to the archbishops from c. 1340.

The Grove, adjoining St. Mary's, is the likeliest site of the original Rectory Manor House.

St. Mary's Vicarage was originally endowed around 1230.

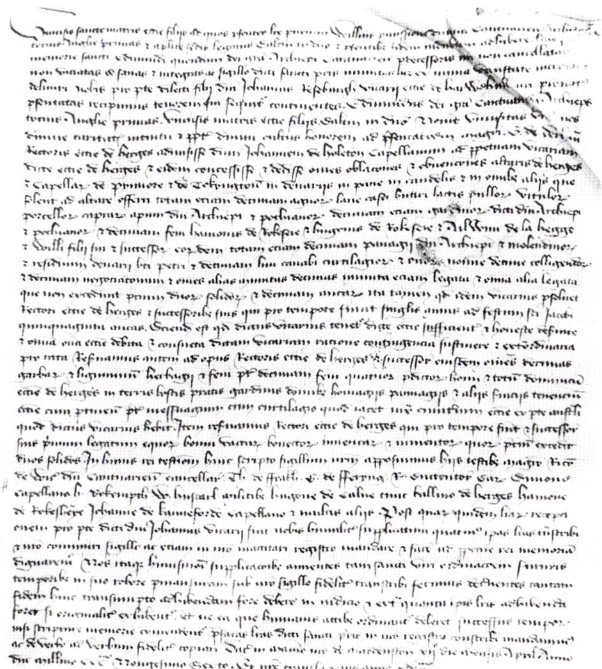

A fragment of the actual endowment admitting John de Holtune as the first vicar of Harrow.

(hence its name) and Wolverton Road.

We also know – by somewhat circuitous means – that Pinner had a chapelry long before the existing church of St. John's was consecrated in 1321. No record of its foundation survives but a reference to "the Chapels of Pinner and of Tokyngton" was found at Lambeth Palace in a document dated April 1396, in which the archbishop of the day, Archbishop Courtenay, confirmed a much earlier grant by his predecessor, Archbishop Edmund Rich (1234–1240), endowing the first vicarage at Harrow.

In other words, there were chapels in existence in Pinner and Tokyngton (Wembley), some time in the third decade of the 13th century.

The Vicarage Endowment, which admits Sir John de Holtune to the perpetual vicarage of Harrow, makes specially fascinating reading in that it precisely records the offerings to be made to the vicar including "all the tithes of lambs, wool, cheese, butter, milk, chickens, calves, little pigs, goats and bees".

Specific mention is also made of produce from neighbouring communities such as "the hay of Hamo de Rokeseie (Roxeth) and Ailwyn de la Hegge (Headstone)", all contributing to a picture of an agrarian way of life that had changed relatively little since Domesday.

Harrow now had three clerics to care for its people for it is known that, around 1200, the Archbishop (who would have been an occasional visitor only) created a separate and subsidiary Rectory Manor at Harrow whose Rectory Manor House was almost certainly on the site of the house adjoining St. Mary's now known as The Grove.

The early rectors, however, would themselves have been pluralists, holding several livings, and it was presumably to correct this somewhat unsatisfactory situation that the additional appointment of a vicar – with his own vicarage – was made.

There is every reason to suppose that this first vicarage was in exactly the same position on Church Hill as today's building – nevertheless one question still remains unanswered.

Where did the early archbishops reside when holding court at Harrow? Since a number of letters written by both King Edward I and King Henry III still survive bearing a Harrow address, it must have been a place of some substance capable of entertaining royalty.

Informed opinion now favours an archbishop's residence somewhere in Sudbury but, in truth, its location has yet to be established beyond doubt. Happily, the mystery comes to an end in 1344 when, incontrovertibly, the archbishop of the day acquired the present Headstone Manor as his palace.

Still standing, though in ruins, the second of the three parish churches of Great Stanmore was built in 1632.

Sir Edmund Flambard, whose memorial brass is dated approximately 1370, was in charge of the forces raised by the City of London to aid Edward III in his Scottish wars.

5. Poverty, Pestilence and Prayer

It must have called for a tremendous act of faith to consecrate new churches in Pinner in 1321 and, around the same time, at Great Stanmore, for these were truly terrible times for the common man.

Edward II's reign, which was soon to end in his uniquely hideous murder, was notable for its violence and treachery. There were more people on the land than ever before but not nearly enough cultivated land to support them. To make matters even worse, a series of natural disasters occurred, including exceptionally poor harvests in 1320 and again in 1321, this time accompanied by an unusually virulent form of cattle and sheep disease.

Nevertheless Archbishop Winchelsey, on one of his well-documented visits to his Harrow Manor, must have seen the need for a bigger and better church in Pinner and set in motion the lengthy process which, in 1321, resulted in the dedication of a church to St. John The Baptist (substantially the same church that has been in use for the past 678 years).

Around this time, too, the profession of a simple, almost child-like faith led directly to the creation of a new kind of chapel with a new kind of priest – the chantry.

A chantry was essentially an endowment, usually of land, from which the income was used to pay a priest to say masses daily for the soul of the founder in particular and the souls of the departed in general. It was a role quite separate from that of the parish priest; indeed, it was not even under his jurisdiction.

A Chantry of Our Lady was founded in the year 1324 by the then Rector of Harrow, William de Bosco, who endowed it with a house and about 100 acres of land in what we now know as Hatch End.

We know, too, that the first chantry priest was one Thomas Akyn but, at this juncture, we cannot be entirely sure whether his chapel was actually within St. Mary's. If so, it may well have been housed in what is now known as the parvise, a little room above the south porch only recently restored for use as an occasional chapel. Certainly, the traces of old, possibly medieval, painting on its ceiling and the presence of a 14th-century incised slab on its floor provide evidence of possible chantry use.

The Victoria County History also records the existence of other medieval chantry chapels independent of Harrow church, including one belonging to Bentley Priory, possibly on Weald Common, and a hermitage dedicated to St. Katharine on Sudbury Common.

If life during the first decades of the 14th century was rarely easy, it was soon to become a great deal grimmer. In 1348, rat-infested ships arriving at our ports brought a truly horrendous pestilence. Known to contemporaries as "The Great Mortality" and, later, passing into history as the Black Death, it is said to have claimed the lives of at least a third of the population of England as well as creating havoc in many other countries of Western Europe.

St. John's, Pinner, was already over 480 years old when this drawing was done in 1807.

The tiny room above the south door of St. Mary's may well have been a chantry chapel. As the picture shows, it was used as a store-room until recently restored for private prayer.

No records survive of its impact upon Harrow but it can scarcely have been any less calamitous than its effect upon nearby Kingsbury in whose manor court rolls reference can be found to a number of dilapidated houses left unrepaired "for fear of disease".

This understandable abandonment of tenements that had once housed pestilence victims is known to have led to a shift of centre in many villages and may be among the reasons such a movement appears to have occurred in Great Stanmore.

In a very real sense, too, even the survivors fell victim for, when the cost of labour inevitably rose with the shortage of man-power, a cruel Statute of Labourers was imposed, preventing all negotiation over wages.

England, moreover, was still engaged in a war with France (the so-called Hundred Years War), which was to drag on into the next century. To meet its cost, increasingly high poll taxes were imposed in 1377–80, prompting the well-organised Peasants' Revolt of 1381.

Given that the revolt was mainly centred in south-east England, Harrow's poor must surely have been involved in the violence that followed, not least in the murder of Archbishop Simon Sudbury.

Sudbury was also Chancellor of England at that time and thus held to blame by the rebels for much of their suffering. Despite the bravery of the 14-year-old King Richard II in meeting the rebel leader Wat Tyler face-to-face and in agreeing to many of the rebels' demands, Tyler's men dragged the Archbishop from the Tower of London and promptly beheaded him on a log on Tower Hill.

In the rampage that followed, many valuable documents were destroyed as the rebels regarded manuscripts such as court rolls as a hated record of their bondage. F. R. H. Boulay in his scholarly "Lordship of Canterbury" suggests that this mob not only plundered and fired many of the manorial records held at Lambeth Palace but also those retained at Harrow.

One local man who, initially at least, prospered from the Peasants' Revolt was Sir William Brembre a city wholesaler who, some ten years before, had been granted estates at Roxeth after their owner, William of Roxeth, had been outlawed for felony.

Brembre whose name is still recalled – albeit with a slightly different spelling – in today's Brember Road, not only refused to panic when London was overrun by Wat Tyler's men but subsequently formed a King's party in the City to consolidate Richard's hold on the throne. His reward was to be elected Lord Mayor of London on three separate occasions. He was, too, at one time Collector of Customs for the Port of London, working alongside a certain Geoffrey Chaucer.

Later, however, his increasingly militant involvement in the politics of the day prompted him to be charged with 39 offences against the realm. Although he boldly claimed a knight's privilege of trial by combat, this was denied him and he was subsequently hanged at Tyburn in 1388.

Surviving Harrow court rolls make several references to Brembre and his estates, none more interesting than the fact that he had failed to cleanse certain of the ditches on his Roxeth land. This may hardly seem a serious offence until one recalls that, within the lifetime of many, that same land had been horribly scourged by the Black Death.

The Pye House, as it looked in 1795.

Church Fields, now public open space leased from Harrow School, were once home to the town's busy markets and fairs.

6. Medieval Fairs and Markets

In concentrating on the troubled affairs of kings and popes and archbishops and on the ravages wrought by war and disease, it is all too easy to paint the distant past as a time of unmitigated gloom. Yet common sense alone should remind us that life for the ordinary man was not without its modest pleasures, such as the weekly markets and annual fairs held in Harrow as early as 1261.

At a time when the average villager rarely travelled far from home, such markets provided a unique opportunity for them to buy and sell and barter a variety of goods.

For the Lord of the Manor, too, they provided a useful way of augmenting the Manor's income through the many market tolls.

So we can be reasonably certain that Harrow's Lord welcomed, first, Henry III's granting of an annual fair and weekly market in Harrow and, secondly, Edward III's somewhat later charter of 1336 permitting the same privileges "at the manor of Pynnore".

As Jim Golland points out in his unique study of Pinner Fair, *Fair Enough*, such charters may simply have been a means of giving legal status to already existing events, in which case both fairs may be older than we think.

Although it may seem odd to us in these more secular times, the early fairs usually combined business and pleasure with some form of religious observance, often connected to the patron saint of the place concerned.

Since Harrow's church was dedicated to St. Mary, the Harrow Fair was originally held on the vigil, feast and morrow of Virgin Day. Similarly, the original Pinner Fair coincided with the patronal festival of Pinner's church named for St. John The Baptist.

Unfortunately, then as now, markets and fairs alike attracted the occasional unscrupulous trader and it was often found convenient to set up an adjoining court-house, where some form of on-the-spot justice might be dispensed.

The system, which had apparently been in use in Normandy before the Conquest, was known as the Court of Pied Poudreux. This Norman French phrase is usually translated as "dusty footed" which, given that the events were invariably held on rough, open land (such as Harrow's Church Fields) would have been an apt enough description of those taking part.

Not only was there just such a court-house in Harrow, it has – unknown to most of our residents – actually survived in an alleyway off West Street.

There are, it has to be admitted, many reasons for this seeming neglect. First, the phrase "pied poudreux" seems to have proved difficult for local tongues and, by the 18th century, prints of the building invariably called it by the more simple name of The Pye House.

Then, after the discontinuance of the fair in 1871, no one seems to have objected when E.S. Prior, the noted local architect, virtually concealed the court-house from view by building the still-extant red-brick Mission House in West Street.

Next, in 1896, the Harrow Electric Light Company put up an early electricity sub-station on its other side, effectively hemming it in.

Finally, over the past 30 years, the Mission House as well as the adjoining court-house itself has been used by a plastic components factory, whose caring owner occasionally opens up the premises to interested visitors.

Today, the court-house is at least protected from demolition by an official Grade II listing; nevertheless its use as a store cannot help but seem an inappropriate fate for what is, after all, the second oldest building on the Hill.

7. The Raising of the Spire

In the roll call of Harrow's history, the year 1450 resonates with particular force and clarity.

For it was in this year that our borough gained perhaps its most significant and certainly most recognised feature. It is, of course, the spire of St. Mary's church which, nearly 550 years after its erection by Rector John Byrkhede, not only dominates the skyline from many parts of the borough but also features on a multiplicity of material put out by local organisations.

Who then was this John Byrkhede, in whose debt we all remain?

He was one of those often despised pluralist rectors of Harrow, but one who obviously came to love the place which shared his time with churches at Wigan in Lancashire and Hawkhurst in Kent.

Earlier in his career, Byrkhede had been Steward to Archbishop Henry Chichele and, in this role, had helped him purchase estates for the foundation of All Saints College, Oxford. Presumably, he had also sanctioned the use of many of Harrow's oaks for the actual building of the college, for a court roll of the Manor of Harrow dated 1445 records that our woods were "grievously devastated by reason of the timber having been felled". There may even have been some kind of deal between rector and archbishop because, two years previously, Chichele had granted the people of Harrow remission from the normal market tolls, an act now commemorated in one of the clerestory windows at St. Mary's recording major events in the history of the church and town.

Obviously, not all of Harrow's oaks were sent to Oxford for Byrkhede now began an ambitious rebuilding at St. Mary's. Although the erection of a splendid spire atop the existing tower was the plan's most exciting feature, Byrkhede also took the opportunity to raise the nave by the addition of a notably fine clerestory. He then added the superb carved roof over the nave and transepts which remains one of the great glories of St. Mary's.

Not surprisingly, Byrkhede chose to be buried within his fine new building where a brass, depicting him in an intricately embroidered cope, was set in the chancel floor. He can hardly have imagined, however, that 550 years later, this cope would be lovingly copied by a gifted needlewoman, Rosemary Priestman, for festival use by contemporary vicars. At other times, the cope reposes in a glass case in the north transept for all to admire.

One of Byrkhede's successors as Rector of Harrow, Prior William Bolton, has also gained a somewhat curious reputation as a local builder.

Bolton, in the manner of the times, was not only Rector of Harrow but also Prior of St. Bartholomew's, Smithfield, which, for several centuries, had owned the Manor of Little Stanmore.

As Prior of Smithfield, he was horrified to learn of an astrologist's prediction that, in

According to his memorial brass in the south transept of St. Mary's, George Aynesworth c.1488 married three wives who gave him a total of 14 children.

Stone coping beneath the spire still bears the name of churchwardens John Osman and William Greenhill, presumed responsible for 17th-century restoration work.

Left *Hannah Putnam, who took over as plumber when her husband died re-leading the spire in 1823, has her name inscribed on lead sheeting, now displayed in the tower.* Right *Erroneously known as Prior Bolton's Tower, this 16th-century armada tower stood in the grounds of St Dominic's School until demolition in the 1960s.*

February 1524, the Thames would overflow with a catastrophic loss of life. Bolton was not alone in his fears and, by all accounts, there was a mass exodus from London to the heights of Highgate and Hampstead.

Bolton, it is said, chose instead to come to Harrow where he reputedly built himself a fortified tower. Until its demolition in 1968, there was, in truth, just such a tower in the grounds of the old St. Dominic's Convent, now a Catholic Sixth Form College.

Many pictures and writings, especially those dating from the 19th century, actually refer to this structure as "Prior Bolton's Tower" but contemporary expertise claims it as an Elizabethan armada tower, one of the tall structures built on high ground throughout the country to enable warnings to be given of the approach of an enemy armada.

Whatever its origins, the tower's loss is a matter for regret and one wonders whether, in today's more conservationist climate, attempts would be made to repair it rather than to raze it to the ground.

As for Prior Bolton, he almost certainly engaged in some form of building at Harrow, particularly as the relatively peaceful reigns of Henry VII and Henry VIII encouraged the development of a comfortable domestic life not possible in more troubled times.

Most probably, Bolton simply extended his Harrow residence for, as we shall read later, this was soon grand enough for one of his successors, the notorious Richard Layton, to offer his mentor Thomas Cromwell "a dozen beds in the parsonage".

The Thames, of course, did not overflow as predicted, but the astrologers seem to have had a ready answer for those who complained at their inaccuracy.

Of course, the month was right, they declared. It was just the century they got wrong. Wait until February 1624, they argued, and it will all come true!

Lavish cape once worn by Rector John Byrkhede
has recently been copied from the vivid detail revealed in this memorial brass.

The last of Harrow's Archbishops, Thomas Cranmer, was obliged to surrender the Harrow manors in 1545.

8. Henry VIII and his Heirs

The fact that Harrow's most prominent inn throughout the centuries has been the King's Head – and that the king depicted has always been Henry VIII – has prompted many stories seeking to link that notorious monarch to our borough.

Again and again, we can read that the inn was once Henry's hunting lodge, even that he courted Anne Boleyn there.

Yet one looks in vain for even a scrap of historical evidence; indeed, there are no printed references to the inn earlier than the 1700s, two centuries after Henry's reign.

But if Henry never favoured Harrow with his presence, he nevertheless had a significant impact upon our town – as upon every other town where there were men to pray and churches to pray in.

On Henry's accession in 1509, it has to be remembered that all such churches were fully Catholic churches with a rite very little different from that practised in all churches in Western Christendom. At that time, too, the Archbishops of Canterbury were Lords of the Manor of Harrow as they had been since AD 825.

Under Henry's rule, however, all this was to change – ironically, not so much from religious conviction as from marital disenchantment. Henry's first wife – and they were married within days of his accession – was the Spanish Princess Catherine of Aragon, who had previously been married to his late brother, a mere boy of 15 at the time of this earlier ceremony.

Initially, at least, Henry's marriage was a happy one but the eagerly awaited son, born in 1511, died in infancy and, after a sad succession of still-births and miscarriages, the only surviving child was a girl, Princess Mary.

By this time, too, Henry had fallen genuinely in love with the attractive Anne Boleyn. Confident that she would give him the son and heir he desired, he seems to have convinced himself that a Papal annulment of his first marriage would be equally good for king and country. He even suggested that his first marriage had offended Holy Scripture and that the Pope might well have exceeded his temporal authority in permitting him to marry a woman who was, in fact, his brother's widow.

This, in itself, was hardly likely to endear him to the Pope but Henry, in his ardour, also made another miscalculation. Catherine's nephew, the Emperor Charles V (who naturally sided with his aunt) was one of Europe's most powerful rulers and one the Pope was most unwilling to upset.

So when the Pope sought refuge in procrastination, Henry heeded the advice of his Chancellor, Thomas Cromwell, that the only clear-cut solution to his dilemma would be for England to break away from Papal allegiance.

Though the full story makes fascinating reading, suffice to say here that Henry ultimately declared himself Supreme Head of the Church of England. He thereby triggered an era of reli-

Though long associated by name with the centuries-old inn on the Hill, no record survives of Henry VIII actually enjoying its hospitality.

gious persecution and intolerance that encompassed not only his own reign but those of his three children, Edward VI (born of his third wife, Jane Seymour), Mary (the daughter of Catherine of Aragon) and Elizabeth (child of Anne Boleyn who subsequently perished on the block).

With Thomas Cromwell at the helm, Henry now set about the dissolution of, first, the smaller religious houses and, then, the greater monasteries, both acts being carried out in a wholly unscrupulous way to ensure that most of their treasure found its way to the Crown.

In 1545, Henry obliged his erstwhile friend, Archbishop Thomas Cranmer, to surrender to him the Harrow Rectory Manor and, subsequently, the Archbishop's Manor.

Similarly, the dissolution of the Priory of St. Bartholomew at Smithfield (which, over the years, had acquired both Great and Little Stanmore) saw these Stanmore lands also pass to the Crown.

Soon all the manors were in the hands of influential members of the laity.

The Archbishop's Manor went to a royal favourite, Sir Edward North, who had been made Chancellor of the Court of Augmentations of the Revenue of the Crown, and thus managed the vast monasterial revenues.

As for the Rectory Manor of Harrow, this passed to Christ Church, Oxford, possibly after some behind-the-scenes manipulation since the last Rector of Harrow and the new Dean of Christ Church proved to be the same man, Richard Coxe.

Meanwhile, in Great Stanmore, Jeffery Chambers, Chief Steward of St. Bartholomew's, got himself appointed as Surveyor and Receiver-General of the self-same Court of

Augmentations in which role he personally took out a lease on the Great Stanmore Manor. He then sold part of it to Pedro de Gamboa, a Spanish mercenary. On Chambers' death, Gamboa was granted the whole of the estate but failed to live long enough to enjoy it, being murdered on the streets of London.

After being held by a series of leaseholders, the estate passed to Sir Thomas Lake, a family name destined to be well known in Stanmore history. As Lake, who became Secretary of State to King James I, was already possessor of the Manor of Little Stanmore, the two manors were now united.

To return to King Henry's day, Harrow was to play a particularly shameful role in the continued despoilation of the monasteries through its then-Rector, Richard Layton, who now undertook the leadership of the so-called Visitation of the Monasteries (in effect, a cloak under which the King could discover the full extent of ecclesiastical revenues).

Layton was a protégé of Thomas Cromwell and his closeness to his mentor is revealed in a letter in which he invites Cromwell to stay at the Rectory House in Harrow. With its reference to "20 beds in the town where there has been no sickness this year and a dozen in the parsonage", this same letter also provides us with an intriguing hint of both the healthiness of Harrow and the actual size of the Rectory.

Layton, too, provides a sad footnote to our chapter on Thomas Becket for it is claimed that he was personally responsible for the desecration of Becket's Canterbury shrine during which the martyr's bones were burned and the shrine's treasures plundered.

Although he remained Rector of Harrow until his death in 1544, Layton appears to have leased the Rectory in 1539 to Thomas Wriothesley, later Earl of Southampton and father of the Henry Wriothesley who was to become William Shakespeare's patron, close friend and dedicatee of some of the sonnets.

It has to be admitted that, although it began so badly, Henry's "reformation" of the Church did bring some genuine benefits to the laity. In 1536 he ordered that an English Bible – as distinct from the traditional Latin one – should be placed in every church, chained to a lectern or reading desk. Two years later, it was decreed that every parish should keep a register of baptisms, marriages and burials. For its safe keeping, every vicar was also instructed to provide a coffer with two locks and keys "whereof the one to remain with you and the other with the Warden".

Later, Henry's daughter, Elizabeth, laid down further instructions for the proper presentation of the registers. Henceforth, it was ruled, all registers were to be made of parchment and, where necessary, the content of the old book was to be inscribed in the new.

This last rule, which came into force in 1559, was unquestionably followed at Harrow for the first volume of the Harrow Registers is, indeed, a parchment book and commences with details from the previous year, 1558; the records from 1538, however, were not transcribed as ordered, possibly because they were no longer available.

The first entries in the surviving registers of Stanmore parish church were made in 1599; those at St. John's, Pinner, said to be in an excellent state of preservation, seem to have been kept in full only from 1622.

With King and Archbishop scornfully trampling on symbols of Papal authority, this frontispiece to a History of the Reformation clearly evokes the religious climate of the day.

9. Catholic and Protestant

To appreciate the problems that beset the God-fearing people of Harrow in the second half of the 16th century, it has to be remembered that, of Henry VIII's three heirs, the first, Edward VI, was brought up a fanatical Protestant and that the second, Mary, was equally rigid in the Catholic beliefs of her mother, Catherine of Aragon.

Both reigns proved comparatively brief, so many people must have lived through the excesses of both monarchs, yet little if any evidence survives of local reaction to such events, suggesting perhaps that the ordinary man felt it safest to bend with the prevailing wind.

Although Henry VIII may be said to have pursued a fairly moderate course in the so-called Reformation of the Church, Edward – only nine when he came to the throne – was easily swayed by those who wished to establish England as an unequivocally Protestant state.

His reign was thus marked by the most extreme forms of Protestantism. First, all religious shrines were pulled down and their relics destroyed. Next, an order was made for the removal of all images that might encourage superstition which, in the event, meant that even humble parish churches lost priceless medieval wall paintings and windows.

Needless to say, the extremists saw evidence of superstition in the most innocent of objects and churches were further stripped of superb manuscripts and other priceless possessions.

A bill for the suppression of chantries followed and, since intolerance often went hand in hand with greed, all chancery property was confiscated.

A further assault on church possessions was made in 1551 with the appointment of a commission to the shires for the express purpose of seizing all available church plate "to be employed unto his highness' use".

Judging from surviving inventories, neither St. Mary's at Harrow nor St. John's at Pinner owned much of real value at that time. Of course, many items might have been previously confiscated although historian Walter Druett advances the interesting theory that, learning from experience, the wardens had by now safely hidden any important possessions that remained.

The same commission also ordered a record of "howselling" people – that is those old enough to take communion – which showed a total of 1000 for Harrow and 300 for Pinner. If we add the likely number of children, it is reasonable to believe that their population was at least one third higher than these figures suggest.

These, of course, were the same people who were about to experience further turmoil for, when the always sickly Edward died at 15 in 1553, he had already been persuaded that the salvation of England lay with a Protestant heir. Thus, he had signed a document to alter the succession in favour of Lady Jane Grey, granddaughter of Henry VIII's younger sister.

As history – and many a play and film – has recorded, Lady Jane reigned only nine days, losing her head for her presumption.

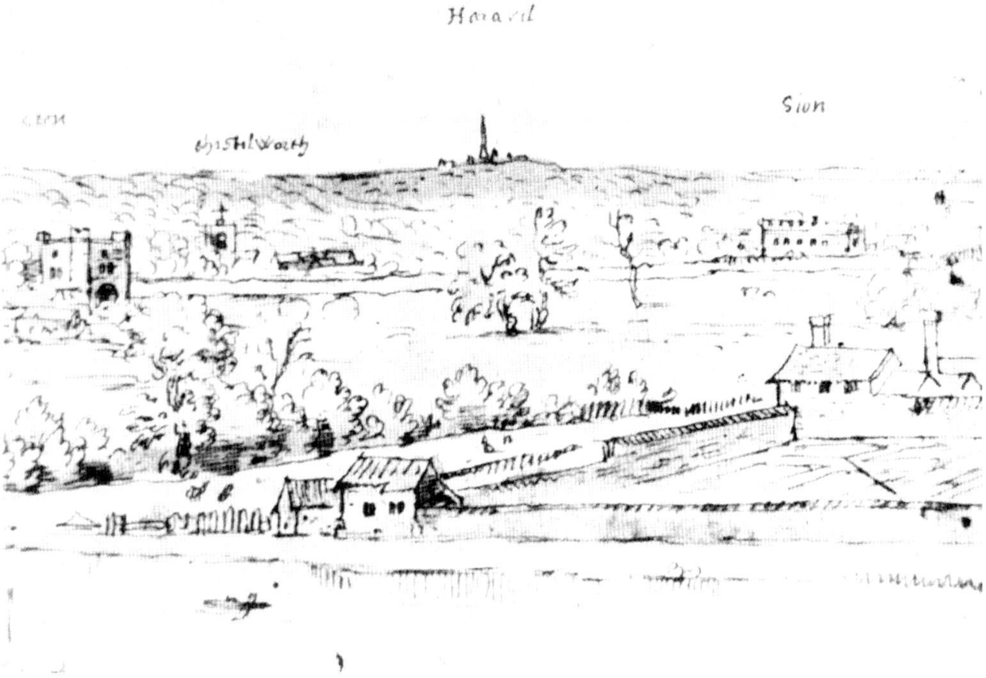

Harrow (shown here as Haravil) owes its earliest drawing dated 1562 to the greed of Spain's Philip II who commissioned views of Mary Tudor's possessions before agreeing to their marriage.

Harrow's church and school can both be glimpsed in this French-drawn panorama of the Thames dated 1643.

Mary duly ascended the throne and set about repealing virtually every ecclesiastical act of the previous quarter-century, aided by those who had either disapproved of the earlier changes – or more likely, disliked the men who had made them.

For all that any kind of religious opposition was met with the most repellent use of force, the people of England seem to have been at least as concerned about Mary's plans to marry the widower Philip II of Spain. The prospect even prompted a rebellion in Kent, led by Sir Thomas Wyatt whose followers managed to cross Kingston Bridge en route for London before they were halted.

Philip seems to have regarded the forthcoming nuptials with a singularly predatory eye, commissioning portraits of all of Mary's palaces so that he could see just what he would be acquiring.

In the event, a distant view of Richmond Palace by the Dutchman, Anthonis van den Wyngaerde, had the happy result of providing us with the first recorded glimpse of Harrow's skyline.

As the illustration on page 38 reveals, Wyngaerde sketched, under the caption Haravil, a small community complete with church and spire sitting on a hilltop roughly half way between Isleworth and Syon.

The royal wedding, which took place at Winchester Cathedral in July 1554, lost Mary a great deal of public sympathy and, when Philip persuaded her to enter the war with France as an ally of Spain, lost her Calais as well. It was England's last remaining possession in France – and a blow Mary was never to forget.

With Philip constantly absent in Europe, Mary turned more and more to her half-sister Elizabeth despite having locked her in the Tower for an alleged but never proven involvement in the Wyatt Rebellion.

In 1558, childless and heart-broken, Mary died. Elizabeth succeeded – and a new and more glorious era in our history began.

Harrow School's own tribute to its founder is a plaque at St. Mary's commissioned c1815 from the famous sculptor John Flaxman. The three boys supposedly represent the sons of Spencer Perceval, the recently assassinated Prime Minister.

10. The Foundation of Harrow School

In 1572, the 14th year of Queen Elizabeth's reign, Harrow acquired an institution which, like it or not – and there have always been contrary opinions – was destined to become the aspect of local life best known to the world outside.

This was, of course, Harrow School, founded – or, to be more precise, re-founded by one John Lyon with the help of a Charter granted by his monarch.

All the evidence suggests the existence of an earlier school on the Hill, not least the presence since AD 825 of the archbishops, who would surely have insisted upon some proper form of schooling for the youth of the Manor.

Many documents, too, point to an earlier school's activities, even to its precise location. For example, a court roll of Harrow Manor, dated May 1475, actually makes reference to a school "inside the churchyard" while, almost one hundred years before, we can read of a manorial tenant called John Intowne being punished because "he delivered his son William into remote parts to learn the Liberal Arts". This might, of course, have signified the righteous anger of the Lord of the Manor on losing the labour of a healthy young man but it may also have been a rebuke to Intowne for choosing to ignore the purely local school.

From the mid 1500s on, more substantial evidence can be found. In 1567, the records of Caius College, Cambridge, note the admission of a boy called Richard Gerard, described as being "of Harrow, Middlesex, School".

Most fascinating of all is the existence of a letter from G. Roper, a son of a trusted royal servant, in which he claims that, on being orphaned c1556, he and his brother were sent "to Harrow to school and were there till we were almost men". His patroness, moreover, was no less than Queen Mary Tudor herself, which suggests that this earlier school was important enough to have come to royal attention.

Why then was such a school in need of re-foundation? – quite possibly, because the severance of the traditional links with Canterbury (as recorded in Chapter 8) may have cut off its primary source of funding. John Lyon's principal motive may therefore have been to put the school back on its feet by providing what he saw as a reasonable endowment.

Lyon, usually described as a "yeoman farmer" of nearby Preston (then part of the widespread parish of St. Mary's) was what we would now call a man of property, owning lands in Middlesex, Bedfordshire, Hertfordshire and Essex. Certainly, he set about his task in a way that would be instantly familiar to any 20th-century entrepreneur.

Bearing in mind that he first wished to obtain a Royal Charter for his school, he sought the assistance of the highly influential Sir Gilbert Gerard whose brother, William, then lived at the great house, Flambards, on Harrow Hill.

Gerard, who seems to have been the uncle of the Harrow boy admitted to Caius, was not

This charming farmhouse, rebuilt in the 17th century on Tudor foundations, was the home – and probably birthplace – of John Lyon. John Perrin Place, Wembley, now occupies much the same site.

Slightly damaged, the figures of Harrow School founder John Lyon and his wife Joan can be seen on this memorial brass in the nave of St. Mary's.

only Elizabeth's Attorney General but something of a royal favourite. Help was also sought from a Ruislip resident, Dr. John Caius of the Cambridge college that bears his name, and with such influential support, Lyon quickly received royal assent to the school's foundation.

His Royal Charter is actually dated the nineteenth of February in the 14th year of Queen Elizabeth's reign which, by our normal reckoning, means the year 1572. The Tudor year, however, began on Lady Day (one of the four traditional Quarter Days, falling on March 25) so the date was still 1571 by the calendar of the day and it is this earlier date that is now commemorated by the school.

Though Lyon gave meticulous instructions on just about every aspect of the school's establishment and subsequent conduct, successive centuries witnessed two unexpected developments that were to provide endless controversy.

The first was the actual value of Lyon's endowment. Of the estates he left for charitable purposes, it was the land in Marylebone and Paddington (which he had assigned to the upkeep of the road between London and Harrow) that proved the most valuable and history records a whole series of clashes on this topic between the School Governors and the Turnpike Trustees, whose responsibility it was to maintain the road.

The second was a gradual but inexorable shift away from the founder's original intention which, as detailed in the Charter itself, was to provide "a certain grammar school...for the perpetual education, training and instruction of boys and youths of the said parish".

Though the economic realities of a less-than-adequate endowment must have played some part in the subsequent changes, several of John Lyon's own statutes must bear an equal responsibility.

For a start, Lyon had always insisted that the schooling at Harrow should be strictly classical with Latin as the primary language not only of tuition but of conversation; indeed, he actually decreed that "None above the first form shall speak English in the School except when they are together at play."

Such a ruling, however scholarly and well intentioned, was hardly one to be imposed upon local lads destined to follow their fathers into trade or agriculture. As one parishioner subsequently put it: "A son educated at Harrow would neither have the taste nor the qualifications to proceed with the business of a butcher."

So, when the local families fought shy of enrolling their sons, it was only natural that the school authorities should invoke another of Lyon's statutes to the effect that "The Schoolmaster may receive over and above the youth of the inhabitants within this parish so many foreigners as the whole number may be well taught and applied and the place can conveniently contain."

Even more significantly, the same ruling declared: "And of those foreigners, he may take such stipend and wages as he can get".

Soon, the fee-paying "foreigners" were outnumbering the free local scholars, a situation which, as later chapters will reveal, was constantly challenged by the many who felt that

Lyon's original wishes had been cruelly betrayed.

But this is to leap ahead in the history of a school whose first building – the so-called Old Schools – did not arise until 1615, years after the deaths of both Lyon and his widow, Joan.

The two Lyons are buried at St. Mary's where, to this day, their memorial brass can be seen mounted on a pillar in the nave. It shows two adult figures only but, from a lithograph of the brass made in the 1840s, we can see that originally it also bore the outline figure of a child.

This is now generally accepted as a representation of a child who died either at birth or in infancy, although the parish registers of St. Mary's, in fact, bear no record of any such birth in the Lyon family.

In the circumstances, it is interesting to conjecture that, had this child been male and survived into manhood, the extent of Lyon's charity might have been very different – and the Harrow we know today might, in consequence, have been a very different place.

11. The Plot against Elizabeth

For all that Good Queen Bess was the most peripatetic of monarchs, our borough cannot lay claim to a single plaque that reads "Queen Elizabeth Slept Here". It is even doubtful whether we could point with assurance to a single visit throughout her 44-year reign.

Yet one of the most serious threats against her life – a plot ultimately designed to place on the throne her Catholic cousin Mary, Queen of Scots – had its eventful climax in our midst.

The story is a complex one and, to appreciate it fully, we need to recall yet again that Elizabeth was King Henry's daughter by Anne Boleyn and, thus, illegitimate in the eyes of the Vatican which had never recognised Henry's divorce from Catherine of Aragon.

At this period, too, there were many who felt that Mary had a legitimate claim to the English throne, being a great-granddaughter of Henry VII by his daughter, Margaret, who had married James IV of Scotland.

Among these loyal supporters were the Bellamy family who lived at Uxendon Manor which, although several miles from Harrow, was still very much within the parish of St. Mary's. Moreover, entries in the parish register during the early years of Elizabeth's reign show that the senior members of the Bellamy household, William and Katharine, paid at least lip service to the current rules of the Anglican Church.

In fairness to Elizabeth, it has to be said that she was disinclined to enforce her Protestantism – certainly not with the extremism with which Mary Tudor pursued her Catholicism – until the Pope of the day virtually forced her hand.

Encouraged by the seeming success of a northern rebellion in the name of Mary (which, in fact, was quickly put down), the Pope – now Pius V – felt it appropriate to stage a formal trial of Elizabeth in absentia. To no-one's surprise, she was both excommunicated and deposed, her subjects being absolved from their oath of allegiance.

Such effrontery, as it was seen by most Englishmen, simply served to unite the majority of Elizabeth's subjects even more firmly behind their monarch which makes the subsequent actions of the Bellamy family all the more dangerous – and courageous.

Whatever they avowed in public, there is no doubt that, in private, the Bellamys not only held true to their Roman ways but also allowed their house to be used as what we would now call a "safe house" for Catholic recusants. As such, it was in particular demand once William Allen had founded a college overseas – by a striking coincidence in Douai, now twinned with Harrow – for the express purpose of training Catholic missionaries to England.

One of these, Father Richard Bristow, subsequently lived quite openly at Uxendon Manor, passing himself off as Cousin Springe, a poor relation of Mrs Bellamy. The deception seems to have been so convincing that, when he died at Uxendon Manor (presumably of natural causes), the Protestant Vicar of Harrow actually buried him at St. Mary's under his assumed name.

The Royal Charter granted to John Lyon bore this impressive seal showing an equestrian portrait of Queen Elizabeth.

The Queen Elizabeth statue which currently looks down from the side of Harrow School's Speech Room is in fact a 20th-century addition to a 19th-century building.

Possibly the Bellamys felt that luck was running with them for, following the death of William Bellamy, the younger members embarked on an even more dangerous adventure. In 1586, they gave shelter to Anthony Babington, the principal figure in the so-called Babington Plot, whose aim was the assassination of Elizabeth followed by the crowning of Mary, Queen of Scots.

The latter was then being held, virtually incommunicado, in Fotheringay Castle. In the hope of uncovering treachery, Sir Thomas Walsingham, Elizabeth's Secretary of State and, in reality, spy-catcher-in-chief, turned a blind eye to the establishment of a secret communications channel whereby letters for the Scottish Queen were smuggled into the castle along with the regular deliveries of beer.

As he had doubtless anticipated, Walsingham did not have to wait long before treasonable material appeared. This was a letter from Anthony Babington to Mary in which he spoke of six noble gentlemen willing to kill Elizabeth on her behalf.

A nationwide hunt for these conspirators quickly ensued. For a while, they seem to have lived off the land but, then, according to the contemporary writer William Camden, "being constrained by famine (they) went to an house of the Bellamy's near Harrow Hill who were greatly addicted to the Romish religion. There they were hid in barns, fed and clothed in rusticated attire."

Other contemporary reports suggest that a suspicious constable actually came to the door of Uxendon Manor but was persuaded to leave by the second son, Jerome Bellamy, who stoutly denied any knowledge of the traitors.

On the eighth day of the hunt, however, the house was surrounded by Walsingham's men and Babington, his four companions, and two of the Bellamy sons were all taken prisoner.

Babington and his confederates died peculiarly hideous deaths which the Queen had ordered "to be protracted to the extremity of pain".

Jerome Bellamy was tried as an accessory, convicted and also barbarously done to death at Tyburn whose name, of course, survives in our local Tyburn Lane – then, as now, en route to Marble Arch where such executions were performed.

Bartholomew Bellamy, another son, was apparently put to the rack so brutally that he died in prison even before he could be brought to trial. The by-now aged and infirm Katharine Bellamy was imprisoned, first, in the Fleet Prison and, then, in the Tower, where some time later she too died. Yet another son, Robert Bellamy, was already in prison at the time of the conspiracy. Subsequently, he was reported to have died by his own hand, a scarcely convincing story given the strength of his religious beliefs.

Even the Bellamy servants did not escape "examination", one Richard Mascall confessing that he had been sent to guide the fugitives and to bring them bread. Some half a dozen Harrow men and women, most in their twenties, were similarly questioned. We know their names. Sadly, we do not know their fates.

As for Mary, Queen of Scots, history records that Elizabeth who, as Anne Boleyn's daughter, had constantly lived in the shadow of the rack and the block, finally permitted another woman – and, more importantly, another queen – to be executed at Fotheringay in February 1587.

Harrow's Parliamentarian sympathies during the Civil War may well have saved St. Mary's carved roof from the vandalism seen in many other churches.

12. The Century of the Civil Wars

Given the relative stability and prosperity of the reign of Elizabeth and of her successor, James I, Londoners now had the time, the money and the inclination to think of building country houses to be used – as a contemporary report recalls – "for their recreation in the summer time and for withdrawing places in the time of common sickness".

Middlesex in general – and Harrow in particular – proved such a popular location that, by 1614, the noted playwright Ben Jonson could people his play *Bartholomew Fair* with characters such as Master Bartholomew Cokes "a tall young squire of Harrow on the Hill" and Mistress Grace Wellborn "of that same place", confident that his London audience would readily identify with them.

Coincidentally, Charles William Hart, the eldest son of William Shakespeare's sister, Joan, also lived locally and is, indeed, buried at St. John's, Stanmore, as requested in his will, although the site of his grave is now lost.

We know, too, that William Gerard (whose family, as we have seen, helped establish the present Harrow School), lived in some style in the great house Flambards on Harrow Hill. Around 1580, he sought to improve its facilities by laying a lead pipe from the house to bring water from the existing town well at the top of West Street. Possibly some deal was struck for the good of the town for, at the same time as a Rectory Manor Roll licensed his domestic improvements, he was also permitted to enlarge the well and erect a pump-house "for the use of all the tenants of the manor to draw and fetch water".

In Stanmore around 1604, Sir Thomas Lake (who, as we have read, owned the two Stanmore Manors) rebuilt the Manor House of Canons, named after the Augustinian Canons of St. Bartholomew's Priory.

His descendants were later to prove good friends to Stanmore, endowing a local school which served the community for some 200 years and building the Lake Almshouses which survived until relatively recent times on land adjoining St. Lawrence, Whitchurch.

Another Sir Thomas Lake was also among those generous residents who donated land for the building of a new church to replace the medieval foundation.

Although one of its tombstones – that of Baptist Willoughby, Rector from 1563 to 1610 – has survived in the garden of a house in Old Church Lane, little is known about the demolition of the old church nor of its removal to a different site.

By contrast, we have considerable knowledge of the building of the "new" brick church which still stands – albeit in ruins – in the grounds of the present St. John's.

Much of this knowledge stems from the fact that two nationally important figures were closely associated with its construction.

One was Sir John Wolstenholme, at whose sole expense the church arose; the other was

Late 18th-century drawing of the long-since-demolished Uxbridge building where Charles I signed the Treaty of Uxbridge in 1644.

King Charles' ill-fated Archbishop, William Laud, consecrated the now-ruined Stanmore Old Church in 1632.

William Laud, later to become Archbishop of Canterbury to Charles I, who performed the consecration ceremony, as his personal diary testifies, on Tuesday, July 17th 1632.

Sir John, a successful merchant whose family had come to Stanmore from Lancashire around 1540, was a man whose vision was at least the equal of his fortune. Apart from his many gifts to Stanmore, he helped finance the New World exploits of both Henry Hudson, who in 1610 sought the legendary North West Passage linking the Atlantic and the Pacific and of William Baffin who set off to explore northern waters in 1615. In the event, Wolstenholme had his name immortalised by both explorers – first, in Cape Wolstenholme at the entrance to Hudson Bay and, secondly, in Wolstenholme Sound and Wolstenholme Island off Baffin Bay in northern Greenland.

His memorials at Stanmore are equally felicitous. Although he was nearly 80 when he died, the inscription above his effigy, now to be seen in the present St. John's, claims that he died "alas too young".

By dying in 1632, Wolstenholme was at least spared involvement in the horrors that, just ten years later, overtook his country and his church.

This was, of course, the first of the Civil Wars that so cruelly set Englishman against Englishman as either Royalists or Parliamentarians.

The problems – political, religious and social – that brought about such strife are far too complex to enumerate here. At the heart of the conflict, however, lay the inescapable fact that, some 20 years after a queen who could do nothing wrong (Elizabeth), England had a king (Charles I) who could do little right and an archbishop (Laud) who, many believed, was deliberately attempting to Catholicise the Anglican Church.

In the circumstances, the ever-strengthening Puritans (those Protestant clergy and laity who desired a more simple service and ritual) began to ally themselves ever more closely with the Parliamentarian opposition to the King.

Some evidence of local opposition can be seen as early as 1635 when Charles unwisely attempted to pay for the upkeep of the Navy by imposing the already unpopular Ship Money on inland as well as coastal counties. In Harrow alone, it is recorded, the King's collectors were obliged to take 40 distresses (that is, the holding of property against debts) from people who simply refused to pay.

We should therefore not be too surprised that, when the first of the two civil conflicts broke out, Harrow proved to be firmly Parliamentarian, not least because Sir Gilbert Gerard, the current occupant of Flambards, was not only an admirer of Oliver Cromwell but had also married Cromwell's first cousin, Mary Barrington.

Although Gerard managed to raise a local regiment on Cromwell's behalf, not all the local gentry shared his political views. Both Sir Francis Rewse of Headstone and Sir Richard Page of Uxendon stood firmly for the King.

As for King Charles himself, legend has long placed him at Harrow in the closing stages of his reign. To this day visitors can read a plaque on the walls of Harrow School's Art School

Smoke belches from buildings along the Thames waterfront in this curious souvenir of the Great Fire of London. Its unknown Italian artist includes a somewhat squat St. Mary's church in the background.

Though the well commemorated by this plaque at the top of Harrow's Grove Hill genuinely existed, its royal links are more suspect.

at the top of Grove Hill claiming that, at this spot, the King watered his horses while taking his last look at London before his capture and trial.

Until the building of the school boarding house, Rendalls, in 1859, this part of the Hill did, indeed, hold a well that was traditionally known as King Charles's Well yet not one of the authorities on the life of the King fully confirms the story. Add the fact that the plaque was not erected until 1925 – almost 300 years after the event it supposedly commemorates – and the whole episode is best regarded as romantic speculation rather than historic fact.

What is undeniable, however, is that the battle lines came worryingly close to Harrow, one battle being fought at nearby Brentford. Later, the building that became the Old Treaty House in Uxbridge was chosen as the meeting place between commissioners appointed by the two sides to consider England's future.

Long before the war's end (and the King's execution in January 1649), Archbishop Laud was impeached. Ironically, during his trial, Sir John Wolstenholme's "building" at Stanmore was cited as evidence of one of many occasions on which the Archbishop allegedly "outwent Popery in the consecration of chapels". Laud was able to claim, rightly, that this particular building was no rich man's chapel but a true parish church. But this one denial was insufficient to save him and he was put to death in 1645.

By a curious coincidence, Laud's personal ivory chalice, used to administer the last rites before his execution, later came into the possession of the local Page family and passed through marriage to a Mr Young of Sudbury Grove. In 1859, it was proudly shown by the Rev. William Oxenham, a Harrow Master, to a meeting of archaeologists held in the school's Old Speech Room.

Parliamentary troops were often cruel and predatory. The 19th-century local historian Ethert Brand, for example, found a parchment in the archives of the House of Lords in which Margery Pope, a widow, petitioned the Lords "in her great extremity and that her deeds, goods and estate may be restored to her".

Apparently, within three months of her husband's death, the Parliamentarians billeted on her demanded £100. When she claimed she was unable to pay because "she had not yet received a penny of her jointure", some thirty men "in a most barbarous manner broke into her house and carried thence the bed whereupon she lay, hangings, brass, pewter and other goods, even all she had". The outcome of this particular incident is not known but we do know that Sir Francis Rewse of Headstone who found himself on the losing side was fined a sum so far beyond his means that his estate had to be sequestered. Indeed, the aftermath of war when Oliver Cromwell assumed the title of Lord Protector and Head of State, proved as dangerous as the war itself, especially to many of those in Holy Orders.

On the very day that Laud died, the Commons (which had already introduced the Solemn League & Covenant binding all adult parishioners to the latest Church revisions) abolished the Book of Common Prayer.

In its place, they brought in the so-called Directory. Henceforth, this was to be the only legal service book but its harsh provisions – among them, the abandonment of all forms of symbolism in a sacred context, even a ring in marriage – were abhorrent to many.

Just where Harrow's vicar, Thomas Launce, stood is hard to assess but, having presumably signed the Covenant, he may well have found the Directory more than he could stomach; certainly, in 1645, he was ejected from St. Mary's and replaced by the Rev. Thomas Pakeman.

At a time when many pulpits were simply seized by ambitious men with no ecclesiastical authority, Pakeman was, at least, an educated man and properly ordained. He was also held in high esteem by Sir Gilbert Gerard who arranged for him to have, in addition to his clerical role, "the instruction and boarding of several children of persons of quality". (There may, of course, be some link here with Harrow School where tuition had begun some thirty years earlier.)

Pakeman's good relations with Gerard may also have helped spare St. Mary's from the worst of the attacks on so-called "idols" that took place elsewhere although, admittedly, some persons at some time in history seem to have defaced the apostles carved into St. Mary's fine timbered roof.

The St. Mary's situation was, to a large extent, repeated at St. John's, Pinner, whose curate, the Rev. John Willis, seems to have clung to office from 1622 to 1641 when presumably his loyalty to Archbishop Laud caused the good folk of Pinner to seek a replacement.

To this end, they petitioned the government that "they may have the liberty to make choice of a lecturer whom they will maintain at their own choice". In seeking not a preacher but a "lecturer", Pinner was demonstrating a typical Puritanical gambit for it had long been recognised that the man in the street was more readily swayed by the demagogue who made strong appeals to his emotions and, especially, his prejudices than by a conventional preacher.

Pinner duly got its lecturer in the person of one Phillip Goodwyn although, initially at least, the Rev. Willis managed to keep him out of Pinner's pulpit!

On the day of Goodwyn's appointment, Willis apparently "expounded in church the whole of one Sunday afternoon until Goodwyn took to his heels".

Obviously such ploys could not be repeated too often and, in any event, Willis was ultimately ordered by the government to give way.

Having got what they desired in the matter of a lecturer (now one William Rowles), the 1649 Survey of Church Lands reports that the people of St. John's "think it very convenient and humbly pray (considering the distance of the place and the illness of the way) that the Chapel may be made a parish church entire of itself".

This time their petition met with no success although it is interesting for us to know that a movement to separate the Pinner church from the mother church of St. Mary's, Harrow, actually began well over one hundred years before the final severance of 1776. The quotation is equally fascinating for its reminder that, in the centuries before the present Pinner Road was built, the route from the Hill to Pinner was through the fields around Rayners Lane – truly "an ill way" in winter months.

The relationship between the two churches continued to be cool and, in 1664, the Harrow churchwardens sought in vain to levy a rate on Pinner to meet the cost of repairs to St. Mary's.

Pinner then advanced a claim of "immemorial immunity" with such success that the parish register was able to record – admittedly, with some degree of smugness – "this is to testify that we never paid any, nor could they recall any by law, towards the repair of their church or steeple".

With the restoration of the monarchy in 1660 – and Charles II tactfully promising "liberty of conscience" to all Christians – local life had presumably returned to normality when two catastrophes befell the capital, a mere ten miles away.

First, in 1665, the Great Plague claimed as many as 100,000 victims over the summer and autumn months. Thousands, especially from the wealthier classes, fled the city and it cannot be doubted that many found sanctuary in high and healthy Harrow which, according to the previous year's Hearth Tax, had some 81 sizeable properties liable for taxation. The Rectory, for example, had 17 hearths and Flambards an amazing 25.

Then, just as plans were being made to improve the stricken city, large portions of it were engulfed in the blaze forever known as the Great Fire of London.

No local eyewitness accounts seem to have survived; nevertheless it takes no great stretch of the imagination to see dozens of families gathered on top of Harrow Hill and other high points of the town watching the blaze – just as their descendants were to witness from afar the Zeppelin raids of World War I and the Blitz of World War II.

James Brydges, Duke of Chandos, wore his ducal robes for this contemporary portrait.

13. The Building of Canons

It was one of the grandest mansions England had ever seen. Its domestic staff of nearly one hundred once included one of the world's greatest composers. Its finances almost provoked a national scandal.

Yet Canons, home of the Duke of Chandos, survived for less than 25 years and, today, virtually nothing remains but its name, shared by a housing estate and a Jubilee Line station!

The name, in fact, pre-dates the Duke's mansion by many centuries. Although recorded first in 1501 on a lease referring to the manor of "Little Stanmore called Canons", it almost certainly originates in an earlier grant of land made to the canons of St. Bartholomew's, Smithfield.

From 1604 the Canons estate was owned – as mentioned in the previous chapter – by Sir Thomas Lake, Secretary of State to James I, and seems to have come to James Brydges, later Duke of Chandos, in 1696 as part of the dowry of his first wife, Mary, who was descended from the Lakes.

Himself the eighth son of Baron Chandos of Sudeley, Brydges undoubtedly spent much of his adult life compensating for the relative poverty of his childhood; certainly as Paymaster of Marlborough's foreign forces in 1705, he seized upon every one of the considerable opportunities to line his own pockets.

Within years he had amassed a staggering personal fortune yet, when the inevitable enquiry into army expenditure was held, Brydges escaped without censure. Nevertheless he wisely waited until he had relinquished his army post in 1714 before embarking upon his most ambitious venture – the building of a vast mansion at Canons.

There was already a Tudor house on the site but this was considered far too modest. Brydges accordingly called in a succession of architects to create for him an impressive Palladian-style house of some 90 rooms, approached by four equally impressive avenues. That from Edgware was three-quarters of a mile long and had, at its entrance, lodgings for eight former sergeants of Marlborough's Army whom Brydges employed as watchmen.

The 83 acres of walled garden included such features as a specially constructed canal fed from the Spring Pond on the Little Common, a lake, fountains and a picturesque artificial mound known as Bellmount (the forerunner of present-day Belmont).

His first wife having died (after giving him nine children, only two of whom survived). Brydges found a new wife – and hostess – in his cousin, Cassandra Willoughby.

Together, they presided over an establishment, the creation of which had cost something in the region of £250,000, a truly awe-inspiring sum for its day. Certainly, its pretensions earned it as much criticism as plaudits.

Daniel Defoe, in his 1724 *A Tour Through England and Wales*, wrote that "it is vain to

The lavish excesses of Canons are widely accepted as the inspiration for this cartoon dated 1731.

The small house created on the original Canons site by William Hallett now forms part of North London Collegiate School.

The magnificent baroque interior of St. Lawrence, Whitchurch, as it looked some 160 years ago.

Left *Erected almost 100 years after his death, William Powell's gravestone at St. Lawrence, Whitchurch, is stronger on legend than fact.* Right *Contemporary likeness of "The Great Mr. Handel" whose two-year residency at Canons produced many fine compositions.*

Originally the Crane, this coaching inn in High Street, Edgware, was rechristened the Duke of Chandos and bore the name until demolition in World War II.

attempt to describe the building. The whole is a beauty and the inside is as glorious as the outside." The satirist Alexander Pope, however, was far less flattering, penning "An Epitaph On False Taste", in which he mockingly declared "His building is a town, his pond an ocean, his parterre a down."

Although the house had its own domestic chapel, opened in 1720, Brydges also set about rebuilding the church on his estate, St. Lawrence, Whitchurch, retaining little of the original except its tower.

Again, no expense was spared and, within a surprisingly modest exterior, the talents of noted European artists and craftsmen fashioned a monument to the baroque style that remains virtually unique in England.

To many eyes, it appears more like a small theatre than a place of worship, an impression heightened by the fact that the altar (standing beneath an arch and flanked by wooden columns) has the appearance of a stage whilst, at the other end, the duke had built a series of boxes for himself, his bodyguards and his household staff.

It was perhaps only to be expected that so theatrical a setting would be peopled by spectacular performers – and so it proved. As his chaplain, Brydges appointed the multi-talented John Theophilus Desaguliers, already well known for his work in philosophy and for the invention of the planetarium. The duke (Brydges became Duke of Chandos in 1719) also expected his chaplain to work on the mechanics of his water gardens and, according to local legend, a corpse once lay three days in the church for want of someone with the time to bury it.

Today, however, the one genuine star in the spectacular production that was Canons is the composer George Frederick Handel, who succeeded Dr. John Pepusch as Music Master in 1718.

Whilst tradition has tended to over-embellish his residency at Canons, there is no doubt that Handel did, indeed, play St. Lawrence's organ. His two-year stay also produced a number of notable compositions, among them the Chandos *Te Deum*, some eleven Chandos Anthems and a masque *Haman and Mordecai*, later developed as the oratorio *Esther*, which was first produced in the private theatre at Canons in 1720.

Around this time Handel also seems to have written, as part of some Suites de Pieces Pour Le Clavecin, the air now known as "The Harmonious Blacksmith", around which an elaborate but totally fabricated story has grown.

In this story, Handel is caught in a rainstorm and shelters in the forge of the local blacksmith called William Powell. Here he is so struck by the rhythmic clanging of Powell's hammer that he decides to write it into a piece of music.

It all sounds entirely plausible until you realise that Powell (who died in 1780 at the age of 78) would have been no more than a youth when Handel worked at Canons. In addition, it appears that the "Blacksmith" soubriquet was not used until the beginning of the 19th century, being the invention of a music publisher whose father had, indeed, worked in a forge.

That this story has been so frequently retold is largely due to the advocacy of one Richard

Clark who, in 1836, published a book about Handel and Powell. Clark even went so far as to have a wooden monument to Powell erected in St. Lawrence's churchyard. When, some 30 years later, the original had succumbed to decay, the legend of Handel and Powell had so firmly established itself that a subscription was raised to provide a new stone monument – the one we see today.

Visitors to St. Lawrence can also view the superb (and wholly genuine) Chandos Mausoleum where James Brydges, Duke of Chandos rests – with his first two wives – in almost as much splendour as he had lived.

Not only is his effigy full-size (with a full-bottomed wig somewhat incongruously surmounting a Roman toga), it stands atop a flight of steps, at the foot of which figures depicting his first two wives are shown kneeling in humble supplication. Because of family quarrels, there is no monument to his third wife (who outlived him) but, though originally buried elsewhere, her remains also rest at Whitchurch.

As for the mansion itself, it fell almost as quickly as it had risen. Burdened with debts, the second Duke of Chandos decided to sell both the house and grounds. Unable to find a single purchaser, he allowed it to be broken up and sold piecemeal at auction in 1747.

Many of its treasures found homes elsewhere. A statue of George I was temporarily moved to Leicester Square and that of George II continues to adorn Golden Square in Soho. In the same way, carvings done for the library by Grinling Gibbons ultimately found their way to the Victoria & Albert Museum.

At auction, the principal lot went to a London cabinet-maker William Hallett who promptly demolished the mansion, using much of its materials to create a much smaller home on the same site. It was this surviving house that in 1929 was purchased, together with some 10 acres of land, by today's North London Collegiate School.

In 1934 Harrow Council bought part of the original Canons Estate for use as a public open space to be known as Canons Park. Later, another part of the estate, principally the walled kitchen garden, was also acquired as a recreation ground, opened in July, 1937, as the King George V Memorial Garden in memory of the then recently deceased monarch.

Today the historic name of Canons is further perpetuated through the agency of both the Canons Park Estate, whose many roads now include a Canons Drive, and the Metropolitan Railway, who, at the very last minute, changed the name of the station they were building to serve the area from Edgware (Whitchurch Lane) to Canons Park.

Otherwise, all that remains to remind us of this truly amazing episode in our local history are the two entrance columns that still stand at the junction of Canons Drive and Edgware Road.

14. The Early Harrow School

For all that John Lyon left detailed statutes controlling virtually every aspect of the school he had founded, not all of them proved workable in practice.

Possibly the first statute to be challenged was that obliging both the Master and the Usher (his assistant) to live where they taught in the original, and then much smaller, Old Schools. William Hide, appointed in 1628, instead persuaded the Governors to lease him a house in the town – on the site where stands today's Head Master's House (though, in fact, he no longer lives there).

Some 40 years later, the rule demanding celibacy of the Head Master was changed rather than lose the otherwise estimable services of the married William Horne.

Over those early years, equally sweeping changes were made concerning the admittance of boys who, from 1668, included an ever increasing percentage of "foreigners" – that is, boys whose parents were not actually resident in the town.

This, in turn, required the provision of a number of boarding houses whose owners seem to have set their own scale of fees.

A letter from Mrs Anne Nicholas to Squire Edmund Verney of East Claydon, written in July 1682, tells us that whilst the Master's House charged £22 a year, she was paying only £14 "for schooling and diet" for her son, simply because "there is no man to govern the house". Fortunately, as she reassures her correspondent, the boy was "yet so young a woman can very well manage him!"

The letter also tells us something about the status of Harrow School pupils at that date for its writer, Mrs Nicholas, was herself daughter-in-law to a sometime Secretary of State. The Duke of Chandos also proved a good friend to the school by enrolling George Brydges Rodney who numbered among his godparents both the duke and King George I.

Though such distinguished parents rightfully expected masters of the highest calibre, not every appointment lived up to expectations.

The near-notorious James Cox, for example, brought the school perilously close to ruin. It is possible that the Governors had been unduly influenced by the fact that he was the previous Head Master's son-in-law; certainly, they stood by him for some 15 years during which the intake of both free scholars and "foreigners" fell disastrously.

Only in 1746 was he removed from his post because – as the Governors' minutes phrased it – he had "for a good while past lived a disorderly, drunken, idle life and neglected the care of the School".

Far from dying early and destitute, Cox actually lived to 95, when he was buried in Pinner churchyard; moreover, his daughter married a local surgeon and apothecary, Dr. Parr, and produced a son Samuel who, as we shall see, himself became a candidate for the Head Mastership.

Site for the annual Silver Arrow archery contest, shown in a 1769 engraving, is believed to have been a grassy knoll off the present Roxeth Hill.

Schoolboys William and John Mason play an early game of cricket in a picture painted just one year after the Silver Arrow's abolition on safety grounds in 1771.

In the late 1760s, Head Master Robert Sumner found his authority strongly challenged by a certain Dr. Samuel Grasse, whose influential connections meant that he could attract boys from some of the noble homes in the land into the boarding house he ran at No.5 High Street.

Grasse, however, persisted in running the house entirely at his own convenience rather than in the best interests of the school and, when the Governors finally sided with Sumner in the dispute, Grasse chose to close the house down.

Faced with the dilemma of more boarders than boarding accommodation, Sumner then approached six local ladies to open their houses to his boys, thus creating the first so-called Dames Houses. (Mrs Nicholas' experience of a house seemingly governed by a woman, almost a century before, was presumably a one-off situation not readily repeated.)

In the event, many of the Dames were no better at imposing discipline than Dr. Grasse had been, although one house, run by a Mrs Leith and located in the present St. Mary's Vicarage, grew to be the second largest house in the school and survived until 1841.

During Sumner's era, the traditional Silver Arrow archery contest, an annual event first instituted in 1648, became ever more grand and attracted visitors from all over the world. In 1765, the guests even included a Red Indian chieftain, who reckoned that, given the opportunity, he could have out-shot all that year's contestants!

Sumner had allowed a dancing school to be built on the site of the present Vaughan Library and it was here, each year, that the Silver Arrow celebrations reached their climax with a lavish ball given at the victor's expense.

It was some of Sumner's pupils who were largely instrumental in saving the parish church when it was struck by lightning during what a contemporary (1763) newspaper account called "the greatest storm…ever remembered by the oldest person". Although the weather-cock and some 15ft of the spire fell down in flames, the boys were so prompt in raising the alarm the church itself was spared.

Ironically, all the goodwill generated by Sumner's devoted years in office was subsequently threatened by his early death in 1771 at the age of 41.

As his successor, the school desperately wanted the aforementioned Dr. Samuel Parr who was, in the fullest sense, a local candidate. Brought up in Harrow, Parr had made his way through the school as, successively, home boarder, Head of School at 14 and assistant master at 20 in which role, as we shall see in the next chapter, he befriended the schoolboy Richard Brinsley Sheridan.

The Governors, however, appointed their own candidate, the Etonian Benjamin Heath. Predictably outraged, members of the school sent a petition to the Governors declaring that "a school of such reputation…ought not to be considered as an appendix to Eton".

The petition also declared, with more than a hint of threat, that the school would not want "opportunities of showing their resentment".

When the Governors very properly ignored the petition, that resentment did, indeed, erupt into violence, vividly described in a contemporary letter to his parents by the schoolboy Thomas Grimston. "We carried our resentment as far as we thought necessary", he wrote, "which I am afraid you will think a good deal too far."

He then went on to describe how "having first locked the School up (we) ran down to the public inn and drew out Mr Bucknell's chaise – one of the Governors who called us blackguards. We drew it out of Harrow town, hollering all the time and knocking it to pieces with our bludgeons."

Retribution was quick to follow and Benjamin Heath's first action as Head Master was to disperse the school for a week while he expelled the principal rioters.

Among them was the 11-year-old Richard Wellesley, whose parents promptly sent him to Eton.

Here he was subsequently joined by Arthur, his younger brother, who became the celebrated Duke of Wellington.

Thus, through one moment of loutishness, Harrow had lost both a future Prime Minister and the opportunity to claim that the Battle of Waterloo was won not on the playing fields of Eton (as the familiar phrase now puts it), but on the playing fields of Harrow.

The first school building to arise following John Lyon's endowment was a single block Old Schools, pictured here in 1795, some 180 years after its erection.

15. Sheridan and The Grove

At the time of writing, the Royal Shakespeare Company is enjoying considerable popularity with a revival of Sheridan's *The School For Scandal*, but, in truth, there is never a theatrical season without some new staging, somewhere, of a masterpiece from the playwright who came to Harrow as a boy and later returned as a resident.

Like those other great comic dramatists, William Congreve before him and, later, Shaw and Wilde, Richard Brinsley Sheridan was brought up in Ireland, a circumstance that was to create quite a few problems when, at the age of eleven in 1762, he was enrolled as a pupil at Harrow School.

Since his father was an actor, occasionally penniless and always feckless, this meant that the lad was frequently abandoned, far from home, for long periods at a time. Worse still, his school fees were not always paid on time, if at all.

Years later, Sheridan admitted to a friend that he was "a very low-spirited boy, much given to crying when he was alone", a fact he attributed to his "being left without money and not often taken home at the regular holidays".

Against this background, a letter still to be seen in the school archives seems all the more touching. Sheridan, conscious of the poor appearance he was cutting in contrast to his wealthier schoolfellows, felt compelled to write the following to an uncle, Richard Chamberlayne:

"You will not be surprised when I tell you that the course of my present letter is partly my want of clothes for my brown ones are quite gone as I have had them almost a year and those which I have now, being of a very light colour and having met with a few accidents, are not remarkably clean."

Even to us today, it is comforting to know that Uncle duly obliged. Further help for the young Sheridan was also at hand at Harrow for his lively personality caught the attention of the relatively young assistant master, Samuel Parr, who seems to have befriended him.

As if in compensation for his less-than-happy terms at school, Sheridan's years after leaving Harrow could hardly have been more successful. At the age of 24, he wrote the immensely popular *The Rivals* followed in quick succession by the libretto for an admired opera called *The Duenna*. Succeeding David Garrick as the proprietor of Drury Lane Theatre, he earned even greater approval for *The School For Scandal*, completed by the time he was 26.

Somehow, Sheridan also found time to woo the beautiful Elizabeth Linley of Bath, perhaps the most notable soprano of her day, a courtship that involved not only a flight to France, where an unrecognised form of marriage took place between them, but the fighting of two duels on her behalf.

For all Sheridan's easy success in the theatre, a career in politics was fast becoming a more attractive alternative and, in 1780, he became the Parliamentary Member of Stafford. All he needed now was a home not too far distant from both Westminster and Drury Lane.

Playwright Richard Brinsley Sheridan (from a painting by Sir Joshua Reynolds) spent eleven years of his life in Harrow.

Sheridan's stables at the top of Grove Hill, drawn some ten years after the playwright had moved to Mayfair.

Sheridan remained loyal to his tutor, Samuel Parr, when the latter left Harrow to open his own school.

Unexpectedly, given his schoolday memories, he chose the old Rectory Manor House adjoining St. Mary's, now called The Grove. Elizabeth pronounced it "a very pretty place" and soon, her youngest brother, William, was a pupil at the school.

Sheridan, however, remained loyal to his old mentor, Samuel Parr who, having left the School in the unhappy circumstances told in Chapter 14, now ran a small educational establishment at Hatton, Warwickshire. So it was no surprise that, when Sheridan's own son, Tom, came of school age, he was sent to Hatton rather than Harrow.

Although The Grove proved ideal for entertaining – politicians such as Edmund Burke and Charles James Fox were frequent visitors – Sheridan began to find the journey to London irksome and, in 1784, he and Elizabeth moved to the more convenient Bruton Street, Mayfair.

As for The Grove, it was later sold to the Pall Mall bookseller, James Edwards and, around 1820, became the Harrow School boarding house it remains to this day.

In Sheridan's schooldays, the other great house on the Hill was Flambards, where, between 1768–1771, the great landscape architect "Capability" Brown carried out work to the value of more than £12,000 for the owner, Francis Herne.

To the delight of Brown's many contemporary admirers, some of his landscaping, including a lake, can still be seen in the grounds of another historic Harrow School house, The Park, built on a slightly different part of the Flambards estate after the demolition of the original house around 1797.

A small circular wall plaque now reminds Hill visitors of the site of Sheridan's stables.

16. Some 18th-Century Personalities

It seems only appropriate that an age – and a locality – that could produce so profligate a personality as James Brydges, Duke of Chandos, could also contain Daniel Dancer, a miser so notorious that both Charles Dickens and Robert Louis Stevenson found him worthy of their attention.

Dancer, however, was not always the eccentric figure history recalls. Born in 1716, the eldest of four children of a prosperous Harrow Weald farmer, he was at one time both a conventional farmer himself and a respected Overseer of the Poor. Yet, following his inheritance of property that included Waldo's Farm at Uxbridge Road, Hatch End, Dancer's behaviour – and that of his sister who shared his home – became more and more bizarre.

Soon their fields were left fallow to save the expense of cultivation, while the one-and-only horse on the farm was allowed shoes for its hind hooves only. As for their home – Astmiss in Weald Lane – it became so tumble-down that a contemporary account said it "had suffered so much by repair, and still wanted so much, that the most diligent antiquary could scarcely distinguish a bit of the original building".

All the while, the couple were obviously putting money away and, when the sister died intestate, her two younger brothers sued for control of her share. Dancer, however, counter-sued and was granted over £1000 for maintaining her during her lifetime.

After his own death at 78, Dancer's house finally yielded up the many thousands of pounds neighbours had long suspected that he was hiding. Over £2500, for example, was found in a dung heap, some £600 was in a cracked tea-pot and over £200 in the chimney-pot, where it was entirely safe since Dancer never lit a fire, even in winter.

Widely known, even during his own lifetime, Dancer's miserliness gave rise to all kinds of stories about fortunes still to be uncovered; indeed, when the Harrow Weald High Road was being widened in 1937, it is said that locals still searched avidly in the excavated soil in the hope of finding further hidden treasure.

Money, it may be said, was also the driving force in the life of Andrew Drummond, who lived at one of the district's grandest houses, Stanmore Park (later the site of RAF, Stanmore).

Drummond was born in Scotland and it is often claimed that he walked all the way to London with the aid of the stick he so often carried in later years but, given that he came from a titled family, the story seems more romantic than realistic.

Far better authenticated are his years as an apprentice to a goldsmith in Edinburgh and the opening in 1717 of the first banking ledger of what subsequently became Drummonds Bank (and, later still, the Royal Bank of Scotland).

The famous Duke of Chandos of Canons had opened an account with him in 1725 and it seems likely that Drummond's ultimate move to Stanmore was largely a business ploy to

Andrew Drummond and faithful dog, painted by Sir Joshua Reynolds in 1762. The setting is presumably the grounds of Stanmore Park.

bring him – in every sense – closer to his most influential customer.

Drummond also built up an amazing portfolio of clients from the fine and applied arts including the designers Henry Holland and Robert Adam, the painters Angelica Kauffman and John Zoffany and the architect James Gibbs who had worked for the Duke of Chandos at Canons. Presumably this is the reason why Drummond and members of his family feature in several distinguished portraits by Zoffany, Gainsborough, Romney, even the great Sir Joshua Reynolds.

Another noted architect of the day, Sir William Chambers, added a new façade to Stanmore Park where Drummond continued to live for some 40 years until his death in 1769.

The marriage of Andrew's son and heir, John, provides an interesting link with another noted 18th-century personality, Harrow's vicar, the Rev. Walter Williams.

In both instances, their brides were descended from the Beauclercs, who were, in truth, illegitimate sons of Charles II by the actress Nell Gwynn.

Williams, however, has greater claims on our interest than this somewhat surprising marriage for he first came to the district in 1764 as assistant curate at Pinner. After ten years (during which, as we have read, the Pinner chapelry was finally severed from St. Mary's) Williams himself was made Vicar of Harrow. He saw no reason, however, to resign his Pinner appointment.

As a later vicar wryly comments in Druett's *Pinner Through The Ages*, "It is interesting to imagine Williams standing every Quarter Day in Pinner porch and taking money from one pocket as Vicar of Harrow and transferring it to the other pocket as Perpetual Curate of Pinner."

Williams, with the added bonus of his wife's money, was able to disdain the relatively modest St. Mary's Vicarage on Church Hill and reside instead at the grander (and still surviving) Pinner House which they purchased for a substantial £700.

He then set about rebuilding the Harrow Vicarage so that it could be let to Harrow School and, to this day, visitors to the vicarage drawing room can see an inscription carved in the wall that reads "W. Williams built this house".

Although it obviously made economic sense to look after the vicarage, Williams seems to have been among the many Georgian clergymen who allowed their churches to fall into disrepair, often – as at Harrow – through arguments with the Lord of the Manor as to who should bear the cost of the inevitable repairs.

The dilapidation of St. Mary's even reached the pages of the nationally read *Gentleman's Magazine* whose correspondent was equally scathing about the Lord of the Manor and "the proprietor of the great tithes".

"In whichever of these gentlemen the fault lies", he wrote, "I am convinced that neither of them has a stable for their cattle in such a bad condition as the place for the Lord's Table is at Harrow."

On the credit side, Williams seems to have been genuinely fond of St. Mary's bells and the

Left *A rare likeness of Walter Williams, Vicar of Harrow for over a quarter of a century.*
Right *Generally regarded as a work of imagination, this posthumous engraving of Daniel Dancer characteristically shows him clutching a bag of money.*

Stanmore Park, the graceful home of the Drummonds, was demolished in 1938 when the site was acquired for the RAF.

first peal ever to be rung there took place during his incumbency on 7th May, 1780, a fact still testified by an 18th-century board in the belfry.

As vicar, we can only presume that Williams was also a consenting party to the shameful treatment accorded St. Mary's beautiful Purbeck marble font.

Despite the fact that, by the year 1800, this font was already some 600 years old, the churchwardens were allowed to throw it out in favour of what a contemporary report called "a wash-hand-basin-looking-thing".

Another report claims that the original was to have been broken up to repair the roadway but was saved by the prompt action of a woman parishioner, believed to have been Mrs. Leith, then running a Harrow School Dames House in the vicarage.

She placed the font in her front garden, in fact, using it as a flower container, and here it remained until the whole sorry affair was revealed in the pages of the January 1827 issue of Hone's *Everyday and Table Book*. A movement then began for its ultimate restoration to the church.

By then, Williams had died following further confrontations with his parishioners over his right to bury strangers (and to pocket the fees) and the appointment of wardens entirely of his own choosing.

It is perhaps significant that he chose to be buried not at St. Mary's but at St. John's, Pinner, where he was later joined by his wife and their one daughter. When alterations were being made to the Pinner Church in 1950, it was reported that their coffins were still clearly visible in the vaults beneath the chancel.

Pinner, specifically Pinner Place, was the home of another notable mid-century personality, John Zephaniah Holwell, of the British East India Company, after whom the present Holwell Place off Eastcote Road is called.

Though Holwell's name may not be immediately familiar, his experiences are still recorded in every popular history book for he was one of the survivors of the so-called Black Hole of Calcutta, one of the most savage episodes in the colonisation of India.

According to Holwell's account, the Nabob of Bengal, on capturing Calcutta, thrust Holwell and 145 other prisoners into a confined space some 18ft square where they were held overnight. Next morning, all but 23 were found to have died.

Though regarded as definitive in its day, Holwell's "Genuine Narrative" of the atrocity has since been challenged by those who claim it would have been a physical impossibility to imprison more than 64 people in the space he described.

Whatever the number of victims, however, Holwell was undoubtedly very lucky to be alive – and to continue in good health until the age of 98.

Lord Byron, whose Harrow connections began with his arrival as a schoolboy in 1801.

17. Rebellion in the Air

The closing years of the 18th century and the first of the 19th were in many ways a time of change and challenge so, in staging not one but two rebellions, the boys of Harrow School were merely echoing events in the world outside.

In 1783, for example, England had been obliged to sign the Treaty of Paris giving formal independence to her rebellious American colonies. Just a decade later, and uncomfortably close to home, the people of France had also overthrown the monarchy in one of the bloodiest revolutions ever known.

Though not without significance, the Harrow revolts were infinitely more parochial in cause and effect, being triggered, first, by an unpopular choice of Head Master and, then, by his unpopular actions.

On the retirement of Joseph Drury, who had built the school to be the equal of Eton in both numbers and reputation, the boys were confident that his successor would be his nephew, Mark Drury. Yet, once again, the Governors had a candidate of their own, a Cambridge Fellow, George Butler.

To make matters worse, when the succession was put to a meeting of Governors, both candidates received an equal number of votes. The Archbishop of Canterbury (as decreed in John Lyon's Constitution) was asked for a casting vote and favoured Butler, the outsider.

In the disturbances that followed, the schoolboy Byron, who had entered the school in 1801, was a principal player.

At first, he was content to write verses jeering at Butler. Later, he seems to have been implicated in a reckless plan to lay a trail of gunpowder through a passage in the house then occupied by Dr. Butler.

At that time, the panelled walls of the Head Master's House were carved with the names of past pupils and, sentiment prevailing over anger, the boys could not bring themselves to destroy such an historic record.

Three years later, however, Butler had to face an even more serious revolt, mounted, according to the 19th-century historian, Percy Thornton, "under the names of Liberty and Rebellion, such being the motto pasted up in the Fourth Form Room".

Dr. Butler's offence on this occasion was to challenge some of the authority traditionally held by the school Monitors. The school responded by stealing the school keys, breaking open the cupboard where the punishment birch was kept, and damaging the chair in which the Head Master traditionally sat.

More seriously, in an attempt to prevent Dr. Butler informing their parents, the ringleaders blockaded the road to London, allowing neither persons nor mail to pass. "For several days", writes Thornton, "the paralysis of authority was complete."

For all that his appointment provoked a school rebellion,
Head Master George Butler was ultimately reconciled with Byron.

An early 19th-century drawing of the Head Master's House whose panelled walls were threatened by explosives.
The Crown & Anchor inn is seen on the right.

Dr. Butler seems to have handled the situation with both firmness and tact, even earning the commendation of the King, George III, who apparently stated that "no man could have acted better under the circumstances".

The monarch had, in fact, visited the school only four years earlier, having decided – more or less at whim – to drive to Harrow from Windsor. It seems that the King alighted from his carriage not at the school gates but at the adjoining inn, the Crown and Anchor. According to the endearingly gossipy Thornton, the inn's landlord, John Bliss, "thought to exalt Harrow in the good King's eyes by producing a local sprig of nobility – the Duke of Dorset".

The monarch, however, was somewhat put out to find himself in the company of a very small – and probably very nervous – schoolboy duke and it was left to Lord Northwick, then living at The Park in the High Street, to entertain the King in suitably royal style.

As a man of wealth whose walls were hung with works by such masters as Raphael, Titian and Caravaggio, the 2nd Baron Northwick had long been the object of considerable local envy. But, following the iniquities of the General Enclosure Act of 1801, that envy had quickly been tinged with hostility.

At its very simplest, this new Act meant that land traditionally belonging to the people – that is, genuinely common land – was now to be parcelled out among the existing land-owners who, the argument went, would put it to more profitable agricultural use.

In Harrow, as elsewhere, this provoked immediate resistance. One Joseph Sellon not only founded an association to oppose the proposed enclosure but also persuaded over one hundred of the so-called "lesser proprietors" to sign a protest petition.

The chief proprietors, however, got their way and the Harrow Enclosure became law in 1803 although the actual awards were not made, nor the plan published, until 1817.

To nobody's surprise, Lord Northwick emerged as the largest land-owner in the parish, prompting a particularly bitter poem,

"The law locks up the man or woman
Who steals the goose from off the common
But lets the greater villain loose
Who steals the common from the goose."

Similarly, in Stanmore, many acres came into the possession of land-owners such as Drummond of Stanmore Park.

It was undoubtedly a feeling of general disaffection with the gentry, as much as any specific educational grievance, that prompted the parish of St. Mary's to choose this particular moment to take the Governors of Harrow School to the Court of Chancery, alleging various abuses of John Lyon's well-documented intentions for the School.

Initially the parish had sent a Memorial to the Bishop of London claiming that the local boys (who, in any event, were hardly queuing up to enrol) were being squeezed out by well-to-do foreigners. When the bishop replied somewhat cagily that it was not proper for him to interfere without judicial direction, the matter was referred to the Courts.

This early Victorian view is clearly inspired by Byron's claim that the Peachey Stone in St. Mary's churchyard was "his favourite place".

The Park, seen in the 19th century, when it was the home of the seemingly hard-hearted Lord Northwick.

Although judgement was ultimately given in favour of the Governors by the Master of the Rolls in August 1811, the school was undoubtedly shaken by the action and some effort was made to encourage free scholars.

That their number remained low (only three in 1816) must be seen in the context of another statistic – the fact that one half or more of the local families then lived wholly off the land.

For much of the 1820s, it proved a poor living, too, records revealing a disastrous fall in grain prices in 1825 followed, a few years later, by heavy rains that left the wheat mildewed and most of the hay ruined.

Someone calling himself "Captain Swing" – a pseudonym then widely used by agricultural protesters – warned Lord Northwick that he had "ground the labouring man too long" and arson attacks and other minor outbreaks of terrorism followed.

Even those who regarded themselves as gentlemen-farmers found themselves in difficulties, among them Thomas Trollope, perhaps best known as the husband of one noted writer (Fanny) and the father of another (Anthony). A former London barrister, Trollope leased 157 acres for farming from Lord Northwick in 1819 but never made a success of the venture. Admittedly, Trollope brought some of his problems upon himself by building a large house on the land at Julian Hill in the expectation of a considerable legacy from an aged uncle. Instead, this relative married late and produced an heir, leaving Thomas seriously in debt. Later, Trollope was to write that, for the whole of the 17 years of his tenancy, the produce he had grown had been insufficient even to pay Lord Northwick's rent.

Lord Northwick remained unsympathetic to his plight, even accusing Trollope of being the ringleader of a conspiracy against him. Finally, Trollope fled in secret to Belgium whereupon Northwick had his crops distrained.

Northwick, in his role as Lord of the Manor, had control of the living of St. Mary's which in 1811 was purchased (as was entirely customary in those days) on behalf of the Rev. John Cunningham.

Cunningham's letters are somewhat ambiguous about the circumstances of his appointment and it is popularly supposed that the new vicar let it be known that Lord Northwick had been impressed by the quality of his preaching.

As the noble gentleman was not known for his churchgoing let alone for his appreciation of the finer points of pulpit oratory, this provoked considerable mirth locally; indeed, Thomas Trollope, son of the fugitive farmer, once wrote that this story was one that, "no inhabitant, clerk or layman, would have believed in the case of his Lordship if the preacher had been St. Paul!"

But then, as we can read in Chapter 19, the Cunninghams and the Trollopes were long engaged in a feud that all but divided the good people of Harrow Hill.

Relatively youthful portrait of the agriculturalist John Claudius Loudon whose fresh ideas revitalised several local farms.

18. A Link with Napoleon

Harrow would seem to be a curious choice for what would now be called a "summit" meeting of the Napoleonic Wars. Even stranger was the venue – the Abercorn Arms on Stanmore Hill.

Yet in 1814, three years after Vicar Cunningham came to Harrow to begin a fifty-year ministry both controversial and influential, the crowned heads of Europe did indeed meet in this unlikely setting to discuss the future of Napoleon Bonaparte.

The royal party comprised the Prince Regent (later King George IV), the King of Prussia, the Emperor of Russia and Louis XVIII of France, who may have been responsible for the choice of Stanmore since, for some years, he had been living in exile in nearby Aylesbury.

The writer, however, has yet to establish why a public inn was chosen since it is known that the Marquess of Abercorn had invited the royal party to the seemingly more appropriate setting of his Bentley Priory mansion.

Nor does any attempt seem to have been made to keep the meeting secret. In fact, according to the *Morning Chronicle* of April 21, 1814, "the principal part of the Nobility and Gentry of that part of the country, and other persons who could muster a horse, went on horseback a mile out of town to accompany Louis XVIII into Stanmore". The same report tells us that the crowd actually took the horses from the French king's carriage and physically drew him to the Abercorn Arms. Here, in a similar spirit of goodwill, selected persons were even allowed to view the royal visitors through the open door of the inn's assembly rooms.

That the fortunes of the Napoleonic Wars were eagerly followed locally is clearly shown in the contemporary diaries of a Harrow School pupil called William Calverley Trevelyan. These frequently comment on the victories of England and her allies, not least because the boys were invariably given a half or a whole day holiday in celebration.

Young Trevelyan also records that Mr Evans preached a sermon for "the Waterloo sufferers (and) collected £107", a very generous sum for that time. Though the lad maintained his diary almost daily between 1812 and 1815 there are inevitable and, sometimes, rather curious omissions.

There seems to be no mention, for example, of the assassination of the Prime Minister of the day, the Old Harrovian Spencer Perceval, the only English premier to be murdered while in office. Perceval's three sons were pupils at the school at the time of his death and it is often claimed that the boys were allowed to pose for the three schoolboys seen on the John Lyon memorial plaque in St. Mary's which the school had recently commissioned from the celebrated sculptor John Flaxman.

It is also worth recording that the school still possesses a copy of the School Bill (or programme) for 1812 at which one of the Perceval boys was to have recited. Against this item, some unknown hand has written, "Not spoken in consequence of the assassination of his father."

Woodhall Farm, Pinner, as it looked in 1810 following Loudon's many improvements.

The Abercorn Arms on Stanmore Hill, drawn c.1850, some 25 years after its use as a royal rendezvous.

Harrow on the Hill

ASSOCIATION,

FOR

The Protection of Property and Prosecution of Robbers.

AT a Meeting of the under-mentioned MEMBERS of this ASSOCIATION, held the 16th Day of December, 1822,

IT WAS RESOLVED,

THAT the following **REWARDS** be paid for the Apprehension and Conviction of any Person or Persons detected in the Commission of the following Crimes, viz.

For any Person or Persons who shall commit a Burglary in any of the Dwelling-Houses of any of the under-mentioned Persons, Members of this Association,

TEN GUINEAS.

For any Person or Persons who shall commit a Highway or Footpad Robbery, upon any of the said Persons, or any of their Family or Servants,

TEN GUINEAS.

For any Person or Persons who shall steal any Horse, Mare, Gelding, Ox, Cow, or other Beast, of the Value of Fifteen Pounds or upwards, the Property of any of the said Persons,

TEN GUINEAS.

For any Person or Persons who shall steal any Horse, Mare, Gelding, Ox, Cow, or other Beast, of the Value of Ten Pounds or under, the Property of any of the said Persons,

FIVE GUINEAS.

For any Person or Persons who shall steal any Sheep, Calves, Hogs, Pigs, or Poultry, the Property of any of the said Persons,

FIVE GUINEAS.

For any Person or Persons who shall cut or maim any Cattle, the Property of any of the said Persons,

FIVE GUINEAS.

For any Person or Persons who shall steal or destroy any young Trees, or lop the Timber Trees, break or steal any Stiles, Fences, Pales, Posts, Rails, or any Iron-Work, belonging to any of the said Persons, or any of their Premises,

TWO GUINEAS.

For any Person or Persons, who shall rob any Orchard or Garden, the Property, or in the Possession of any of the said Persons,

ONE GUINEA.

For any Carter who shall sell on the Road, or elswhere, any Hay, Corn, Coals, or other Things, the Property of any of the said Persons,

FIVE GUINEAS.

For any Person or Persons who shall receive any stolen Property of any of the under-mentioned Persons, Members of this Association,

FIVE GUINEAS.

The above Rewards to be paid by the Treasurer of this Association, on the Conviction or Convictions of any Person or Persons guilty of any of the above Offences.

F. WINKLEY, Secretary and Treasurer,
County Fire Office, Harrow.

MEMBERS NAMES.

The Rt. Hon. Lord Northwick.	William Smith, Esq.	~~Mr. Thomas Wilshir.~~	Mr. R. Brown.
The Rev. Dr. George Butler.	John Gray, Esq.	Mr. John Gurney, Senior.	Mr. John Bliss.
The Rev. Benjamin Evans.	Archibald Campbell, Esq.	Mr. J. Gurney, Junior.	Mr. G. Kearly.
The Rev. William Drury.	~~Archibald~~ Condall, Esq.	Mr. D. Gurney.	Mr. W. Grainger.
Charles Hamilton, Esq.	Mr. John Read.	Mr. Jason Gurney.	Mr. T. Hodsdon.
George Harley Drummond, Esq.	Mr. G. Watson.	Mr. G. Elmore.	Mr. T. Walker.
John Lee, Esq.	Mr. .. Higgs, Junior.	Mr. T. Foster.	Mr. Archer.

Any Person (whose Residence and Property does not exceed Six Miles from the said Parish) desirous of becoming a Member of this Association, is required to apply to the Treasurer, at Harrow.

HASON, Printer, 21, Clerkenwell Green, London.

Harrow On The Hill Association poster listing its 1822 members including Lord Northwick, Head Master George Butler and John Bliss, licensee of the Crown and Anchor.

The tomb which Loudon built for his parents at St. John's, Pinner, remains famous for its "airborne" coffin.

For all its imperfections, the diary does provide eyewitness testimony to various episodes in the town's history. His comments that "last night a haystack of Lord Northwick caught fire and has not yet done burning" almost certainly refers to the outbreak of agricultural "terrorism" mentioned in the previous chapter. A December 1812 entry also reminds us how Harrow was becoming increasingly lawless for, on that day, "after last church, we were chased by some footpads who had before chased Drummond and Chichester but we got away from them".

In fact, since 1801, Harrow Hill had maintained its own anti-crime organisation called with admirable clarity, "The Harrow On The Hill Association for the Protection of Property and the Prosecution of Robbers". It remained active throughout the first quarter of the century, its functions subsequently being taken over by the newly formed Metropolitan Police.

The end of the Napoleonic Wars witnessed a great wave of affection for its greatest hero, the Duke of Wellington, with roads, buildings and even public houses named in his honour. (Harrow Hill still boasts Wellington Terrace, Nelson Road and Trafalgar Terrace.) The duke's good humour must have been sorely tried by the many demands made upon him, none more curious than a request from the local horticulturist John Claudius Loudon.

Loudon had a great many talents but readable handwriting was obviously not among them. When he wrote to the duke asking permission to view the beeches at the ducal seat of Stratfield Saye, Wellington not only read "breeches" rather than beeches, but believed that the signature (Loudon) was that of the Bishop of London. Imagine then the surprise of the bishop when he received a communication from the duke courteously stating that, while he failed to understand the bishop's desire to see his breeches, he could certainly do so, if he wished.

Apocryphal or not, the tale does put a delightfully human gloss on the career of Loudon who, having trained as a landscape architect in his native Scotland, came south to a realisation that English farming methods were in need of radical improvement.

Consequently, in 1807, he persuaded his farmer-father to take a lease of Woodhall Farm, Pinner. Together, father and son not only transformed the farm house (still existing in Woodhall Drive), but also made such a success of the farm that, within two years, they had leased a second farm at Kenton Lane.

Loudon's subsequent pamphlet on his agricultural methods captured the attention of an Oxford land-owner who invited him to manage his 5000-acre property. Here, Loudon was allowed to take in students and so, in effect, start up Britain's first agricultural college.

Loudon left many legacies including a famous series of encyclopaedias on gardening, plants and trees. He also gave Pinner church its strangest memorial – a large pyramid-like structure from which a stone coffin projects into the air. The fact that it was built in memory of his parents, William and Agnes Loudon, prompted many to believe that the airborne coffin actually held their bodies. Others even believed that it had been built this way on father's instructions in an effort to retain an inheritance to be paid only so long as he remained "above ground".

The truth, as so often, is more prosaic. The structure is best described as an architectural whimsy, if not an actual folly. As for William and Agnes, they are sensibly buried in the vault beneath.

Vicar of Harrow for a full 50 years (1811–1861) John Cunningham knew, as friend or foe, all the great personalities of his day.

19. Cunningham's Alternative School

Having arrived in Harrow at a time of considerable local disaffection with Harrow School, it is greatly to Vicar Cunningham's credit that he was quick to realise the need for a village alternative to John Lyon's Foundation.

Within a year, indeed, he had opened a parish school – in essence, the forerunner of today's Roxeth First and Middle School – on London (later Roxeth) Hill. At the beginning, this was entirely financed by voluntary subscriptions including, in its first year, his own donation of £20 and some £26 he had managed to extract from Lord Northwick. Nevertheless the first year's expenses far exceeded the money subscribed and it seems that Cunningham met this shortfall – and, later, many others – from his own pocket.

That there was a great demand for such a school was quickly proved and, by 1816, a *Digest of Parochial Returns* was able to note the attendance of 120 children at a Day and Sunday School supported by subscriptions. Mention was also made of a Sunday evening school for adults and a Sunday School at Harrow Weald.

Financial assistance was later to come from the recently formed National Society for the Education of the Poor, which also helped to establish National Schools in Great and Little Stanmore around 1826.

Some two decades later, the Great Stanmore Infants School was built at the expense of Miss Catherine Elizabeth Martin of Woodlands, Stanmore Hill. When Stanmore continued to grow (becoming an official Post Town as early as 1829), she endowed the school with a further £1000.

Pinner, too, built a village school at the bottom of the High Street in 1841.

Meanwhile at Harrow School itself, Dr. George Butler had secured himself a modest place in its history by becoming the first Head Master to extend the school buildings. In 1820, Charles Robert Cockerell, architect to the Dean and Chapter of St. Paul's, added a new wing to the original Old Schools building.

Cockerell seized the opportunity to give each wing a new and impressive oriel window looking towards the school yard, thus producing so harmonious a building that today's visitors can scarcely believe that one wing is some 200 years older than its neighbour.

Cockerell also added the cupola and clock, extensively restored as recently as 1998, as well as the impressive flight of steps leading up from the school yard – or Bill Yard, where the boys would congregate for the checking of the school bill (or roll). This was, of course, an especially vital discipline when many boys were lodging in houses, which, as we have seen, had little formal connection with the school's administration.

Around the same time, Head Master Butler also constructed the first bathing-school place on fields off the Watford Road which was to grow from the original muddy Duck Puddle

Cunningham's first school on the present Roxeth Hill was succeeded in 1851 by this charming Victorian building, still in use almost 150 years later.

A rare photograph of Stanmore National School on Stanmore Hill, built in 1854 and demolished in 1971.

to the vast Ducker Pool of living memory.

For all that Vicar Cunningham was made a Governor of Harrow School in 1819, his background as a one-time curate to the Rev. John Venn, the noted evangelical Rector of Clapham, did not exactly endear him to the many High Anglicans of Harrow's teaching staff. Nor was the situation helped when, shortly after his arrival, Cunningham burst into print with a book called *The Velvet Cushion* which, in the guise of the "autobiography" of a pulpit cushion, took a critical and strictly evangelical look at changes in religious practice since the days of Mary Tudor.

Then, in 1822, Cunningham became a central figure in a genuine *cause célèbre* whose reverberations were felt well beyond Harrow.

The innocent cause was the 5-year-old Allegra, illegitimate daughter of Lord Byron (by Claire Clairmont) who, while being cared for in a convent in Italy, tragically died of a fever. Her distraught father, recalling his own happy years as a schoolboy at Harrow, desired that her body be brought back from Italy for burial at St. Mary's where he wished a plaque to be raised in her memory.

It would seem a simple enough request but, of course, the child had been born out of wedlock and Vicar Cunningham felt that any public commemoration of Byron's illicit union would be – as he phrased it – "injurious to the morals of the Harrow schoolboy".

There followed a full vestry meeting attended "by all the masters and sundry of the leading parishioners", at which it was agreed that a private burial be permitted but that no stone be allowed to mark the spot.

Surprisingly enough, the latter decision seems to have been upheld by a succession of Harrow vicars and it was not until 1980 that the Byron Society was granted permission to erect the little stone marker now to be seen just outside the south porch. This was presumably the closest anyone could come to fulfilling Byron's wishes since, 150-odd years after Allegra's death, the exact location of her unmarked burial had long been forgotten.

Henry Drury, Byron's old tutor who performed the private ceremonial, was especially angered by Cunningham's views and neither he nor his family – three of whose members were masters at the school – ever forgave him; indeed, J. Cotton Minchin in his *Old Harrow Days* was to refer to the Drury and the Cunningham families as "Harrovian Capulets and Montagues".

This enmity also undermined the vicar's already shaky relationship with Henry Drury's great friends, the Trollope family, a situation aggravated by the fact that the Trollope fortunes failed as those of Vicar Cunningham continued to prosper.

Having lost his first wife in 1821 (after giving him eleven children), Cunningham had since married the young and monied daughter of General Sir Harry Calvert so, when the Trollopes were obliged to move out of their handsome but expensive Julian Hill home, Cunningham had the means – and, as they saw it, the audacity – to move in.

It is often said that Fanny Trollope exacted a cruel revenge by basing the unattractive cen-

Fanny Trollope, an engraving of the writer looking rather gentler than her reputation suggests.

The original (and still extant) Trollope home on Julian Hill was leased to Vicar Cunningham once the Trollopes had run into financial problems.

tral character of her novel *The Vicar of Wrexhill* on Cunningham. Many contemporaries professed to see the connection and Samuel Wilberforce, son of the great abolitionist, even wrote to a friend complaining that "The Vicar of Wrexhill is meant, you know, for the Vicar of Harrow. It is a most abominable attack."

On an admittedly lighter note, Cunningham is reported to have had a certain amount of trouble with his curates. William Bruce, in particular, is remembered solely for being unforgivably forgetful. The Rev. Richard Harris Barham, remembered as the author of *The Ingoldsby Legends*, recalls how, one day in 1838, he arrived at St. Mary's to do some brass rubbings when he came across a wedding party seeking in vain for a clergyman.

Having taken it upon himself to marry the couple, the Rev. Barham felt equally obliged to leave a little note for the absentee. It read:

"It's a very great abuse, Mr Bruce, Mr Bruce
And you're quite without excuse
And of very little use
As a curate, Mr Bruce."

Given the initial hostility of Vicar Cunningham to her commemoration, Allegra, Byron's illegitimate child, had to wait 150 years for this plaque to be erected.

One of the very first steam trains chuffs past Harrow Hill (top right) in this illustration from a railway book of 1839.

In a slightly later drawing, Harrow's first railway line is shown crossing the still-extant bridge over what is now Headstone Drive.

20. The Coming of the Railway

In 1837 there occurred an event whose importance and influence were to echo down the century, one that is now acknowledged as perhaps the greatest single factor in the development of the town we know today.

The event was, of course, the laying of the very first railway line through Harrow with a stop roughly where Harrow and Wealdstone station stands today.

Given that the existing town was on top of a hill, this was probably as close as the engineers could come although subsequent critics, notably staff and boys at Harrow School, declared a preference for a station on the other side of the Hill closer to Wembley and London.

Although, as we shall see, the arrival of a railway train created great excitement, initial response to the idea of a railway was far from encouraging. Even in the early 1830s, Harrow was reasonably accessible by road from London – and vice versa – as there were two daily coaches to the capital: one left from the Crown and Anchor inn on Church Hill, the other from the King's Head in the centre of the town. Both passed through the toll-gate which, until its closure in 1847, existed on Sudbury Hill near its junction with London (now Roxeth) Hill.

The Paddington branch of the Grand Junction canal also crossed the south-west corner of St. Mary's parish, carrying both freight and passengers. Both services – road and water-borne – were vigorous in their opposition to the new and competitive mode of transport.

In an area noted for the quality of its hay, local farmers were also worried that the railway would depress their prices by bringing in cheaper produce from other parts.

Even many of the landowners, across whose acres the new-fangled "iron horse" would run, were less than enthusiastic until the offer of surprisingly generous sums of money by the London & Birmingham Railway Company quickly won them over. As Lord of the Manor, Lord Northwick seems to have received a staggering £3600 for the sale of just 17 acres.

The actual building of the line was not without its moment of drama, Harrow schoolboys taking exception to the inevitable presence of gangs of itinerant navvies.

As the Rev. Henry Torre wrote in a book of contemporary reminiscences, "The stalwart navvies, many of whom passed through the town to buy baccy and beer...rarely escaped a stone from one of the Harrow boys and their language and bearing, being consequently uncourteous to us, they came to be considered our natural enemies." In the resulting fisticuffs, blood was sometimes splattered on the Head Master's railings "which blood", the reverend gentleman somewhat callously records "did not proceed from the boys".

Once the trains were in service, however, the predominant local feeling was one of excitement. Archdeacon Phelps even wrote in his diary that it was "a great diversion to go down

The Crown and Anchor inn, which for many years adjoined Harrow School's main gate, was a starting point for one of the London coaches.

Road, rail and canal traffic are all depicted in this possibly imaginative 19th-century engraving which clearly shows St. Mary's on Harrow Hill.

to the railway station and see the arrival of a train".

His claim to have seen "about 400 passengers brought up at the rate of 30 miles an hour", merely confirms the foolhardiness of a railway guard called Thomas Port who became the line's first fatal victim when he slipped between the carriages while making his way along his train – on the outside!

Tragic as it was, his end might have been forgotten but for a remarkable epitaph inscribed upon his tomb in St. Mary's churchyard. Written by an anonymous hand with what can only be described as grisly relish, it reads as follows:

"Bright rose the morn and vigorous rose poor Port,
Gay on the Train he used his wonted sport.
'Ere noon arrived his mangled form they bore
With pain distorted and o'erwhelmed with gore.
When evening came to close the fatal day,
A mutilated corpse the sufferer lay."

Five years later, a further station was opened at Hatch End, making the Pinner area even more attractive to wealthy Londoners seeking out-of-town homes.

Although other areas undoubtedly shared the same problem, one drawback to making a home on and around Harrow Hill was the lack of acceptable sanitation.

In summertime especially, we can read that "in every road from the Hill and in the main streets of Harrow itself, there is constantly some bad odour". In times of drought, these problems were further aggravated by a very limited supply of water with which to flush such drains as existed.

Something obviously had to be done and, following outbreaks of cholera in the region of Hog Lane (now Crown Street) in 1847 and 1848, the great and the good took the one course open to them.

Under the terms of the recently established Public Health Act, they petitioned for a public enquiry.

In 1849, this was duly conducted by a notably thorough Superintendent Inspector called George Thomas Clark who held public sessions in the King's Head on two days in July (when presumably the odour was at its most pungent), spending the rest of his time personally inspecting the town.

Clark's report, which can still be seen in the Local History department of our Civic Centre Library, deserves to be quoted at some length since it not only draws a uniquely detailed portrait of Harrow life at that time but also provides a useful corrective to any rose-tinted views we may hold about the past.

"Harrow", he proclaimed, "though called a village, and without a market, is in fact a town which has retained its village government. Its affairs are regulated by two churchwardens, three overseers of the poor and four surveyors of highways."

He notes its fast growth – from 3861 people in the 1831 census to 4627 persons ten years

Prince Albert arrives to open the Royal Commercial Travellers' School, Hatch End, in October 1855 – drawing commissioned by the Illustrated Times.

Some 60 years later, guests assembled in the still-surviving Elliott Hall for Speech Day celebrations.

The original Half Moon at Roxeth Corner was one of 54 inns and beerhouses that had opened on the Hill by 1873.

The Temperance movement felt obliged to open its own local establishments, of which the most successful was the Cocoa Tree adjoining St. John's, Pinner.

On the social side, there were already clubs to join, among them Harrow Town Cricket Club and the Harrow Literary Institute.

The same *Visitors' Handbook* which, somewhat amusingly to our eyes, divides the town's residents into "Gentry" and "Traders", listed no fewer than one hundred names within the latter category.

Many were wholly of their time, including saddle and harness makers, wheelwrights and blacksmiths. Others, such as the tuck-shop owner and straw-hat maker, were largely dependent upon the patronage of Harrow School. Nevertheless the Hill boasted a full complement of the kind of "service" shops so sadly lacking today – for example, three bakers, three butchers, a fishmonger, several grocers and greengrocers, a couple each of drapers, ironmongers and confectioners and at least six boot- and shoe-makers.

The town also had a phenomenal number of drinking places although such statistics need to be viewed against the reality of an age when beer (in moderation) was both cheap and safe, in contrast to the local water supply.

As we have seen, one of the first actions of the newly created local Board of Health was to form a waterworks company to improve the Hill's supply nevertheless conditions elsewhere were much slower to improve. As late as the early 1870s, the Vicar of Harrow Weald was able to state in evidence to a water enquiry that many of his 1100 parishioners were dependent upon filthy ponds. At the same enquiry, a Harrow Weald baker claimed that he had no other water "except that from the roofs of houses".

Although its intentions had been sound enough – to maintain some control over the sale of liquor – the Duke of Wellington's Beerhouse Act of 1836 hardly helped the situation by allowing any householder assessed on the Poor Rate to retail beer on their own domestic premises.

The result was a proliferation of drinking places which by 1873 reached a total of some 27 inns and 27 beer-houses on Harrow Hill alone.

To modern sensibilities, perhaps the most curiously sited was the old Crown and Anchor, right next-door to the gates of Harrow School's principal building, Old Schools. Its proprietor then was one John Bliss and, it is said, that to those older boys who managed to gain entry, his premises were fondly known as "The Abode of Bliss".

A worried school ultimately made the proprietor so good an offer that he happily moved premises to the top of West Street whereupon the original inn was converted into a home for the School Custodian, known to this day as Custos.

At much the same time, others were making valiant attempts to persuade the townsfolk to tread the path of temperance. Around 1861, the Harrow Temperance Association rented a room in Crown Street, which some years later became the Royal Oak Coffee Tavern. By 1885, they claimed 245 adult and 250 junior members and were able to operate a coffee cart in College Road for the benefit of workers on the nearby railway line.

Pinner had an even more famous temperance establishment called "Ye Cocoa Tree" which

Harrow's first local paper was published from the block on the left of this High Street view. As the canopied town well is still visible (right) the picture was taken some time before its demolition in 1880.

Rarely seen pre-World War I photograph of Sheepcote Farm, where Thomas Grimwade patented a popular powdered milk.

occupied a particularly imposing site right next-door to St. John's church. Once a house called Equestrian Villa – owned by the family who drove the Pinner–London coach – it was bought in the 1870s by Judge William Barber who, possibly through shared evangelical zeal, was able to persuade a very distinguished architectural partnership of Ernest George (who later designed Claridges) and Harold Peto (who did much of the interior of the liner *Mauritania*), to transform it for public use. Though it began solely as a temperance coffee house, "Ye Cocoa Tree" soon won a wider reputation for the excellence of its catering and, by the turn of the century, had become a popular rendezvous for "country" excursions by church and school parties.

In March 1855, the town acquired its very own newspaper, originally known as the *Harrow Monthly Gazette and General Advertiser*. A modest 4-pager, in tabloid format, it was published from premises in the High Street, Harrow on the Hill, by William Winkley Jnr., a local estate agent and member of one of the Hill's best known families.

According to its very first editorial, Winkley sought "to meet a need that has been generally felt in this place". His first issue, however, was as much a national as a local paper, possibly reflecting Harrow's interest in the conduct of the current war in the Crimea.

Certainly, he included lengthy reports from the war front as well as a letters column in which one correspondent advocated the erection of a local memorial "to show future generations how gloriously the men of Harrow fought at Alma, Inkerman and Balaclava".

Among the new paper's advertisers was Grimwade's Desiccated Milk, a form of powdered milk patented by Thomas Grimwade who had been farming at Sheepcote Farm since the 1840s.

Having been despatched in vast quantities to British troops in the Crimea, Grimwade's product earned a glowing testimonial from the war's greatest heroine, nurse Florence Nightingale. Writing from Scutari Barracks Hospital in March 1859, she described it as the best substitute for fresh milk she had ever encountered.

22. Harrow's Victorian Statesmen

When the Crimean War began in 1853, England's Prime Minister was the 4th Earl of Aberdeen. At its end in 1856, he had been succeeded as premier by Lord Palmerston, a fact of some considerable interest to our community in that both men were not only Old Harrovians but also maintained a life-long connection with the district.

They were not, as we have read, the first Old Harrovians to assume the premiership.

Predecessors included the tragic Spencer Perceval (assassinated in office in 1812), the largely forgotten Viscount Goderich (1827-28) and the charismatic Sir Robert Peel who first became Prime Minister in 1834, returning to the same high office in 1841.

Apart from his signature traditionally carved on the panels of the Fourth Form Room in Old Schools, the town lacks mementoes of Peel's years at Harrow School, although legend insists that the two boys shown on the memorial plaque to Head Master Joseph Drury in the south transept of St. Mary's, Harrow on the Hill, were actually modelled on Peel and Byron.

The two were, indeed, among Drury's more illustrious pupils, being not only contemporaries but very nearly "birthday twins", since a few days only separated their birth dates.

It was as Home Secretary, however, rather than as Prime Minister, that Peel lodged his greatest claim to fame with the creation of the Metropolitan Police Force.

To this very day, an older generation is apt to speak of the police as "bobbies" – a clear reference to Bobbie Peel. In the last century, members of the force were also known as Peelers.

Of all the premiers to be educated at Harrow – the total to date is seven – it was the fourth, George (Hamilton) Gordon, later the 4th Earl of Aberdeen, who knew Harrow best. He even made his home at the Stanmore mansion of Bentley Priory – see Chapter 27 – following his marriage to the daughter of an earlier occupant, the Marquess of Abercorn.

Today, Lord Aberdeen's effigy can still be seen at St. John's, Stanmore, where he was buried in 1860.

Lord Palmerston, his immediate successor in office, was also said to be "Harrow to the backbone".

Certainly, he was a familiar figure in the town for, as the historian Percy Thornton wrote around 1885, "No school function of importance was complete without Lord Palmerston's presence."

He was, too, a very visible figure for, even in his seventies, it was his custom to ride to Harrow from his home in Piccadilly on his favourite white horse.

This mode of transport, though efficient enough – he was reputed to do the journey within the hour – was not without its problems. According to J. Cotton Minchin in his *Old Harrow Days*, Palmerston rode to Harrow to attend Speech Day in 1864. But, having attend-

Four of the seven Prime Ministers educated at Harrow School within the space of 100 years:
Above *Spencer Perceval, Lord Aberdeen*
Below *Sir Robert Peel, Lord Palmerston.*

The Shaftesbury plaque on Church Hill identifies the spot where, as a schoolboy, the great Victorian philanthropist witnessed a pauper's funeral and was inspired to devote his life to the poor and oppressed.

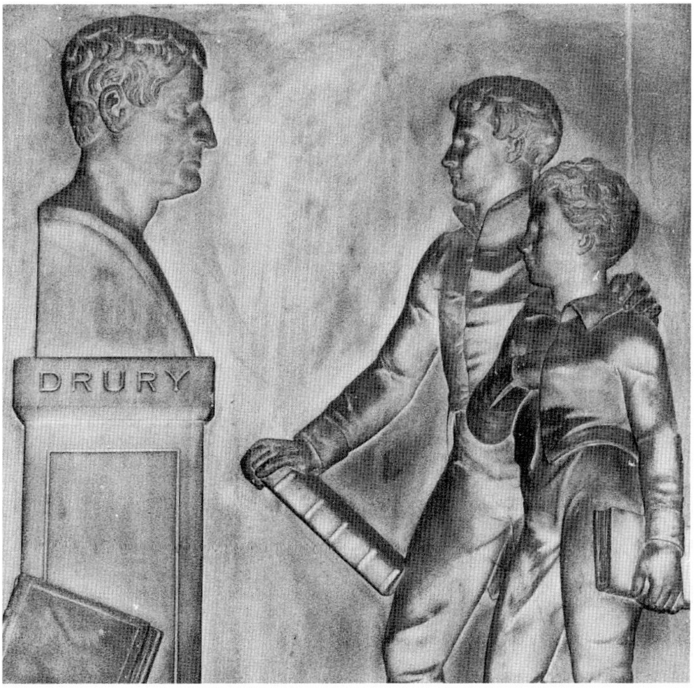

Byron and his school contemporary Robert Peel are popularly supposed to be the boys paying homage to Head Master Joseph Drury on the latter's memorial plaque in the south transept of St. Mary's.

ed to his horse at the King's Head stable, he had so neglected his own dusty and dishevelled appearance that, when he presented himself at the Head Master's House, the staff at first refused him entrance.

The fact that the school was also entertaining the Prince of Wales (later King Edward VII) may well have contributed to this ultra-caution!

A more troubling incident, just a few yards away, is always said to have had a lasting impact on the schoolboy Anthony Ashley Cooper – and thus on the social history of this country.

As recounted by his former Head Master, Dr. Butler, Cooper returned to the School in his old age by which time, as the 7th Earl of Shaftesbury, he had become one of the greatest philanthropists of the age. The statue of Eros, god of Love, at Piccadilly Circus is dedicated to his memory as is Shaftesbury Avenue itself.

Walking on Church Hill, Lord Shaftesbury apparently turned to Butler and claimed that it was at this particular spot that he had been so appalled by the sight of a pauper's funeral, attended only by drunken pall-bearers, that he had determined to devote the rest of his life to the poor and the needy.

Though a plaque on the wall of Old Schools records this turning point in Shaftesbury's life, it remains a fact that the practice of undertakers recruiting pall-bearers, however unsuitable, at the church gates was apparently still rife some 50 years after his schooldays.

A letter in an 1863 edition of the *Harrow Gazette* speaks of the continuing disgrace of hired bearers being "dressed in all colours and frequently in liquor".

Shaftesbury's philanthropy is also recalled locally by another plaque – at Roxeth First and Middle Schools on Roxeth Hill where the still-existing 1851 block arose largely at his Lordship's expense as a memorial to a son who died while a pupil at Harrow.

23. Scandals at Harrow School

On the surface, at least, the middle years of the 19th century were good ones for Harrow School but, in truth, the school's growth was far from untroubled.

The 1850s even witnessed two major scandals of which the first rapidly became public property, spectacularly fuelling the ongoing debate about public school discipline. The second – and arguably far greater – has only come to light in relatively recent times.

At the heart of both scandals we find the forceful, enigmatic and, ultimately, highly controversial Head Master, Charles Vaughan, for whom the Vaughan Library is named.

Born in 1816, Charles Vaughan was a pupil of the famous Dr. Thomas Arnold at Rugby School and, at the early age of 26, his talents brought him tantalisingly close to succeeding the great man as Rugby's new Head Master. (In the event, Rugby's Governors decided by just one vote, that Vaughan was a little too young for so responsible a role.)

Two years later, he was offered the post of Head Master of Harrow, then admittedly at a very low ebb in its fortunes with a school roll that had dwindled to a mere 69 boys. But his strong personality combined with shrewd teaching methods inherited from Dr. Arnold, quickly reversed the decline and, within a couple of years, the numbers had risen to around 200.

Vaughan's success was admittedly helped by the fact that an increasing number of non-Harrow families were now realising that, if they themselves took up residence in the town, their sons could be educated at little or no cost as John Lyon Foundationers.

So, as lads from genuinely local families continued to stay away (in the belief that a classical education was not for them), the school began to welcome even more "foreigners" who were often the offspring of famous parents.

Among them, as we read in an earlier chapter, were the sons of the Trollope family (barrister-turned-farmer Thomas Trollope and his writer wife Fanny); also, Percy Shelley (named after his late father), whose mother Mary Shelley, the creator of "Frankenstein", moved temporarily – and unhappily – into lodgings in Harrow.

Later, the Governors felt obliged to plug this loophole in the statutes by insisting on a qualifying residence of at least twelve months before any boy could be accepted as a pupil.

Dr. Vaughan was also canny enough to realise that some further gesture should be made towards the local boys. With the support of the Parochial and Literary Institute of Harrow, he set to work to create a small commercial school with a limited but adequate curriculum wholly taught in English. Later, when the Governors refused to finance it from normal School funds, Vaughan dipped into his own pocket to bring the so-called English Form into being, initially in a rented coach-house.

Under Vaughan's guidance, the main school continued to prosper and, by the time the roll had risen to 450 or more in the mid 1850s, he was frequently described as "a second founder".

Although earlier hailed as "a second founder",
Charles Vaughan, Head Master of Harrow, was forced to resign in 1859.

Then two heavy blows fell in quick succession.

Vaughan had always been a loyal adherent of the monitorial system, whereby a not inconsiderable share in the maintenance of discipline was borne by senior – and presumably responsible – boys.

In November 1853, it became all too apparent that such powers were being used irresponsibly after a monitor called Platt had punished Randolph Stewart, a son of the Earl of Galloway, with a "whopping" for alleged insults on the football field.

Platt not only chose a thicker cane than usual but also delivered 31 strokes across Stewart's shoulder blades with such ferocity that the boy had to be taken to the school doctor who, quite properly, reported the whole incident to Dr. Vaughan.

As a result, Vaughan deprived Platt of his monitorial status. This, however, was not the end of the matter since, once the boys had told their respective parents, both families complained to school alleging victimisation of their sons.

Furthermore, when Vaughan refused to reinstate Platt as a monitor, the senior Platt took the (at the time) highly unusual course of releasing their correspondence to the popular press who, then as now, were not unhappy to be provided with a stick with which to beat the public school system.

As a loyal Old Harrovian, the Prime Minister, Lord Palmerston, felt obliged to write to Vaughan asking for some reassurance in the matter. This ultimately took the form of an open letter to *The Times* (possibly produced in collaboration with the premier).

To his credit, Vaughan did not shirk the issues involved. He admitted that the tide of public opinion was setting against any kind of corporal punishment; nevertheless he insisted that the monitorial system was "capable of great good and impossible to replace by any efficacious substitute".

Even by his own standards, it was a skilled performance and confirmed the widely held view that Vaughan (who had been in Holy Orders since 1841) was destined for the highest office in the Church.

But this was not to be and for a reason not widely known for at least another 100 years.

For all his undoubted cleverness, Vaughan was foolish enough to become overly fond of one of his pupils, a boy called Alfred Pretor. Even more stupidly, he seems to have committed these sentiments to paper, for Alfred Pretor, boastfully if hardly surprisingly, showed this correspondence to another boy with homosexual leanings, the soon-to-be art critic, John Addington Symonds.

From mixed motives, in which jealousy probably played a part, Symonds set about plotting Vaughan's downfall. On arrival at Balliol College, Oxford, he confessed his secret both to John Conington, who held the Chair of Latin Language and Literature, and to his own father, fully aware that neither man could remain silent in the matter.

Despite the pleas of Mrs Vaughan, a daughter of the Bishop of Norwich, who is said to have gone on her knees to Symonds' father, the latter was adamant that, as the price of silence,

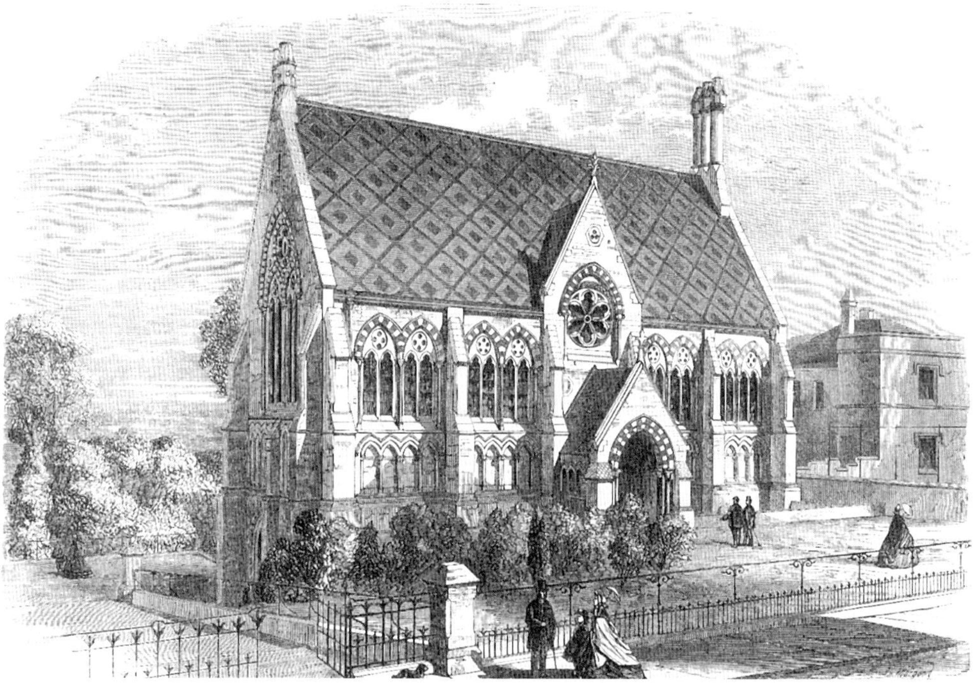

The Vaughan Library, built by Gilbert Scott in Vaughan's honour, drawn for the Illustrated London News of 1863.

A direct descendant of Vaughan's English Form for local boys, the Lower School of John Lyon was opened in Middle Road in June 1876.

Vaughan must leave Harrow immediately. Moreover, he must seek no further advancement in the Church. So it was that the whole world of education was stunned when, in 1859, Vaughan announced his sudden resignation, stating that 15 years of headmastership was as much as a man's strength could stand and quite enough for the welfare of the school he governed.

The Victorians, as we now know, were notably adept at keeping secrets. In the case of Vaughan, the truth may even have been kept from the Prime Minister because, in quick succession, Lord Palmerston actually offered the disgraced man the vacant Sees of Winchester, Rochester and Ely.

For whatever reason – genuine thanks for an otherwise successful headmastership or a supreme act of face saving – the school went ahead with the building of the superb library in his memory, now rightly regarded as one of Gilbert Scott's finest creations. Lord Palmerston even laid the foundation stone although we can read what significance we like into the fact that he failed to stop for the lunch provided. (A possible explanation is, in fact, given in Chapter 24.)

As for Vaughan himself, his constant refusal of high office earned him a reputation for selflessness verging on saintliness and it became the done thing for men training for the ministry to travel to Doncaster (where he remained a humble vicar) to seek his advice and counsel.

Only after the senior Symonds had died did he feel it safe to accept, first, the post of Master of the Temple and, later, that of Dean of Llandaff. In reality, these were relatively minor posts for one whom many had regarded as a future Archbishop of Canterbury.

Two years after Vaughan's departure, the school was faced with another problem although, this time, it was a problem shared with other ancient scholastic foundations such as Rugby, Eton and Winchester. It seems that, just as in Harrow, the good people of these similar communities harboured sundry grievances about the way "their school" had changed over the centuries; so many grievances, in fact, that in July 1861, the government of the day set up a Royal Commission whose job it was to investigate "the revenue and management of certain colleges and schools".

It took three years for the commission's findings to be published and hardly as many days to raise the hackles of the ordinary townsfolk of Harrow.

On the vital topic of free education at Harrow, the commission was quite adamant that "neither public convenience nor respect for the Founder's wishes demand that it should be kept alive". This view was ultimately enshrined in the Public Schools Act of 1868 which officially transformed Harrow into a "public school" – that is, open to the public at large rather than to boys from the immediate locality.

The outcome, however, was not as bad as many feared. Since the commission also affirmed that "some provision should be made out of the revenues of the School for the especial benefits of the class contemplated by the Founder", the Governors looked again at Vaughan's earlier English Form.

With its own building in Middle Road and proper financial support, this re-emerged in 1876 as the Lower School of John Lyon. The rest, as they say, is history.

St. Mary's interior, as it looked before Scott's 1847 restoration. Vanished features include a school gallery (left), a plain east window with reredos in front, high boxed pews and a more elaborate pulpit.

24. The Legacy of Gilbert Scott

It is one of the great glories of Harrow Hill that one of the names most closely associated with its 19th-century rebuilding is not some obscure and long-forgotten architect but the notable Sir George Gilbert Scott; indeed, if anything, Scott's reputation is even higher today in a decade that has witnessed the successful restoration of his inimitable Albert Memorial.

Scott's association with the Hill actually began comparatively early in his career, when he was employed by the vestry of St. Mary's to undertake a massive restoration of the parish church.

Though neither Scott's own writings nor the vestry minutes elaborate upon this early commission, it seems certain that it sprang as much from Scott's standing as a churchman (he came from a long line of men in Holy Orders) as his reputation as an architect. Moreover, Scott's grandfather had been first secretary of the Church Missionary Society with which Harrow's vicar John Cunningham was closely associated throughout his life.

At this date, it is impossible to establish just how much of the work was actually done by Scott himself. It was his deputy John Burleton who first came to Harrow to survey the church and much of the correspondence that survives is signed "in the absence of Mr Scott".

Though Scott was later accused in the architectural press of making virtually "a clean sweep of St. Mary's interior", there can be little doubt that Vicar Cunningham was delighted with the result. Certainly, when a new school chapel was proposed in 1854, Scott was the man they sent for.

Although he was again able to work in the Gothic style he preferred, using flint and stone (as at St. Mary's), he had to build around the existing chapel in a somewhat piecemeal fashion. The building we see today also reflects the work of many other hands, including the 1861 addition of a spire, put up in memory of the long-serving school master "Billy" Oxenham, ironically said to have been a lifelong opponent of any such embellishment.

Around the turn of the century, too, Scott's original chapel entrance, straight off the roadway, was replaced by the present porches on either side. This followed complaints of both dirt and, surprisingly for 1903, of traffic noise penetrating the building!

In 1861, Scott obtained his third Hill commission – the creation of a library in memory of Dr. Charles Vaughan, the Head Master who had retired (in circumstances related in the previous chapter) some two years earlier. By now, Scott felt sufficiently confident to give Harrow one of his most exuberant buildings, all polychromatic brick and fanciful tiling without, it must be admitted, much to link it stylistically to his other local commissions (except perhaps the later Christ Church on Roxeth Hill).

As such, the Vaughan Library was hardly to the taste of the Prime Minister, the Old Harrovian Lord Palmerston. Not only was Palmerston an avowed classicist, he had already clashed with Scott on designs for the India Office so nobody was entirely surprised when, after laying the foundation stone in 1861, the premier declined to stop for the luncheon celebrations.

Scott's chapel (left) and Decimus Burton's 1840 Head Master's House, seen around the turn of the century. The chapel later moved its front entrance because of "traffic noise" while the latter subsequently gained a storey.

Scott's neighbouring masterworks pictured earlier this century: the school chapel (left) and the Vaughan Library.

In the decades that followed, Scott's stylistic flourishes exerted considerable influence upon other architects, such as William Burges who, in 1871, was engaged to build a new Speech Room.

Burges, perhaps best known for the extraordinary interior he designed for Cardiff Castle, had always been a bold innovator with a highly individual vision. He was not, however, a man likely to work in harmony with the school's Building Committee and, when he first unveiled his somewhat unconventional plan for "a classical Greek theatre encased in a Gothic carcass", it is said that the entire committee resigned.

The choice of a difficult site – part of the so-called Hanging Gardens poised between the churchyard and the main road over the Hill – hardly helped; in fact, the sheer cost of driving piles deep into the hillside caused the abandonment of the original plan to incorporate new laboratories and a gymnasium (both of which were built elsewhere by other hands).

Though Lord Abercorn laid the foundation stone in 1874 (two years after the Tercentenary for which the building had been commissioned), a further three years was to elapse before the building opened. Even then, it was still incomplete and important details such as twin spires to complement the existing spires of the parish church and chapel were never implemented.

Although the building we see today may have fallen some way short of the architect's original vision, it still has the power to impress. Additionally, it provided the Hill with an unexpected bonus when the many tons of earth excavated from the hillside were used to create the beautiful Terrace Gardens on the London side of the road.

Many other familiar Hill buildings are the work of Charles Forster Hayward, whose brother was both mathematics master at the school and chairman of the contemporary local Board of Health and thus in a position to put plenty of work his brother's way.

Possibly for this reason – as much as for his undoubted talents – Hayward gave Harrow the large school house called Druries at the foot of Church Hill, the Natural Science Schools and Laboratories, the first Knoll boarding house and the original Garlands, both in Peterborough Road, as well as the so-called New Side to the Head Master's House.

For the town, he provided the first custom-built fire station and Board Office (now an estate agents) adjoining the King's Head and, on the opposite side of the town green, a public hall, later transformed into the Hill's first – and only – cinema.

Much of this new building by Hayward and others was carried out during the headmastership of Henry Montagu Butler, grandson of the George Butler once challenged by Byron. In his day, however, the second Butler's forward thinking met with almost as many brickbats as bouquets. An all-too-typical response was that of George Russell, one-time secretary to Mr Gladstone who, in an autobiographical volume called *One Look Back*, wrote that Butler "with a hundred gifts and accomplishments had no artistic or aesthetic sense and, under his rule, the whole place was over-run by terrible combinations of red and black brick".

Happily, the school proved kinder to its head and the last building to be undertaken before his retirement (a handsome Queen Anne-style block by Basil Champneys) was named the Butler Museum Schools in his honour.

Roxeth's vicar, the Rev. Andrewes, shown with his wife, is buried in Rome near his good neighbour Ballantyne.

Left *Poet Matthew Arnold lived for some years at what is now Byron House in Byron Hill Road.*
Right *R.M. Ballantyne, as depicted in one of the many newspaper eulogies that followed his death in 1894.*

25. They chose Harrow

Even after one has discounted the illustrious roll-call of Old Harrovians, the 19th century still presents us with an amazing parade of literary personalities who, for a variety of reasons, made their home in Harrow.

For some, the magnet was Harrow School; for others, the chance of living in a tranquil and healthy community within what we would now call "commuting distance" of the capital.

The poet, Matthew Arnold, was undoubtedly drawn by a combination of the two. From his correspondence, we learn that he was already looking for a spot close to his sons at Harrow School when he fell in love with the property now called (somewhat ambiguously) Byron House in Byron Hill Road. The fact that it was already some 140 years old was another factor in his choice for, as he wrote to his mother, "I cannot tell you how the old countrified look of the house pleases me."

Harrow town was equally pleased to have him in its midst and the *Harrow Gazette* wrote a most generous welcome to a man who could already make three considerable claims upon its interest – as the son of one of the most famous of headmasters, Dr. Arnold of Rugby, as a noted Schools' Inspector and, above all, as a distinguished English poet.

The school proved equally welcoming and, although he was never to hold any official position, Arnold was entrusted with the welfare of one of its most illustrious pupils, H.R.H. Prince Thomas of Savoy. Apparently related to half the crowned heads of Europe, this lad was actually offered the crown of Spain while still a pupil, earning himself the nickname "King Tom".

As a contemporary was later to write: "He was a popular boy and no-one had the slightest grudge against him; but, for all that, everyone made a point of kicking him in the hope of being able to say in after-life they had kicked the King of Spain. Unfortunately, Victor Emmanuel, fearing dynastic complications, forbade him to accept the crown and so he got all the Harrow kicks and none of the Spanish half-pence."

The story of "King Tom" is, in fact, woven into the otherwise largely fictitious account of School life to be found in Old Harrovian Horace Annesley Vachell's *The Hill*, in its day (1905) a very considerable best-seller.

Several very real tragedies, however, were to overshadow Matthew Arnold's years at Harrow. Thomas, his eldest boy, a semi-invalid, died six months after entering the school (in the same year that the Arnolds lost their infant son). Just four years later, the next son, Trevenen, also died at the school from what appears to have been meningitis.

It was a son's schooling that also brought Charles Kingsley briefly to Harrow in 1874. Kingsley, the noted author of such books as *The Water Babies* and *Hereward The Wake* was Rector of Eversley in Hampshire and it is doubtful whether he would have come to Harrow

Charles Kingsley briefly lodged in the London Road while his son attended Harrow School.

at all but for the insistence of his wife, Fanny.

This lady was convinced that Harrow School was – in her own colourful phrase – "a sea of vice" and gave her agreement to young Grenville's enrolment only on the understanding that both parents would be close at hand. Kingsley was, therefore, obliged to take a house on the Hill; not the present Kingsley House in London Road but a now-vanished property called *Woodside*, elsewhere in the road.

Kingsley was destined to spend very little time there for, shortly after the move, he left for a prolonged lecture tour of America, leaving Fanny a remarkable love letter in which he declared he would "like to spend a week in bed in Harrow with you – but it cannot be".

Nor was it ever to be – for, by the time of his return, Fanny Kingsley had, entirely of her own volition, removed Grenville from the school. "If you saw the boy's exhausted look and poor small face", she wrote, "you would agree that he is wholly unsuited to public school. He hates the place for its wickedness which is indeed surpassing!!!" (The three exclamation marks are Fanny's own.)

It would be nice to report that Grenville Kingsley derived lasting benefit from his mother's care and caution. Instead, he later became involved with a married woman and was promptly packed off to Australia. Here he worked as a sheep farmer until his own relatively early death.

Ironically, while no attempt seems to have been made to mark the home of Matthew Arnold, a GLC Blue Plaque, one of the relatively few in the entire borough, commemorates the residence of R.M. Ballantyne, a writer who is today all but forgotten.

Yet, in his day, Ballantyne was easily the most prolific and successful writer of boys' fiction, most of which recalled his own adventurous youth. *The Young Fur Traders*, for example, was inspired by his early career with the Hudson's Bay Company while books such as *The Coral Island*, *The Dog Crusoe* and *Martin Rattler* drew on other exotic backgrounds and peoples he had encountered.

By the 1880s, however, his adventures were behind him and, with sons to educate, he happily settled, first on Roxeth Hill and later at Duneaves, a house he caused to be built in Mount Park Road.

Here he wrote a further 20 books. Ballantyne also found time to support many worthy causes, including the newly emergent Salvation Army, good work that earned him the friendship of his one-time neighbour, Rev. John Floyd Andrewes, Vicar of the newly-built Christ Church on Roxeth Hill.

Having lived something of a charmed life, Ballantyne had a golden guinea buried in the foundations of Duneaves in the hope of further good luck. In fact, he contracted the rare Ménière's disease which causes uncontrollable giddiness and collapsed and died in Rome, where he had gone in search of a cure.

By an amazing coincidence, his old friend, the Vicar of Roxeth, also died when in Rome and the two friends can now be found only yards apart in the same Protestant cemetery.

Grim's Dyke's third – and most famous – occupant, the librettist Sir William Gilbert.

26. Grim's Dyke in its Heyday

When so many important buildings have disappeared in the borough (and with them their historic connections), it is doubly satisfying that Grim's Dyke off that celebrated viewpoint Old Redding, Harrow Weald, has not only survived as an hotel but also that its management is intent on keeping alive the links with its most celebrated occupant, Sir William Gilbert of Gilbert & Sullivan fame.

Yet Gilbert is only one of a trio of interesting personalities associated with the house.

The first is its designer, Norman Shaw, a highly influential figure in the Arts & Crafts movement who was once a pupil of Charles Cockerell who famously re-built Old Schools on the Hill.

Shaw worked on Grim's Dyke (a name inspired by the possible Iron Age earthwork that runs through its grounds) not for Gilbert but for the noted Royal Academician Frederick Goodall. The latter seems to have been well satisfied with the result for all that, to contemporary tastes, it presents a somewhat idiosyncratic mix of Gothic revivalism with the late Elizabethan style of tall chimneys, red-tiled gables and leaded lights.

Obviously, there was no shortage of money for the commission since Goodall (though less highly regarded today) was one of the most successful painters of his day. The Royal Academy of 1869, for example, included some fifty of his typically exotic oil studies of Egypt, all of which commanded extremely high prices.

For the amusement of his Harrow Weald guests – and for use as models – Goodall even imported herds of Egyptian goats and sheep to graze in his grounds. Ten years later, however, he was telling his friends that it was "a disadvantage for an artist to live entirely in the country" and he sold Grim's Dyke to Robert Heriot, a partner in Hambros Bank.

Heriot lived there for a full ten years so it was not until 1891 that Sir William Gilbert moved in. He was, by then, immensely rich from his contribution to a theatrical partnership which had already produced the unrivalled sequence of still-performed comic operas such as *The Mikado*, *The Gondoliers* and *The Pirates of Penzance*. He was therefore able to adopt the lavish life-style of a country squire in which he was supported by an indoor and outdoor staff of at least twenty servants.

His guests – who included personalities as diverse as the novelist Anthony Hope, the painter John Millais and the singer Liza Lehmann – were both amazed and delighted to find his garden (and sometimes his house) filled with caged birds, lemurs, monkeys, even a braying donkey named Adelina Patti, after the contemporary opera star.

The donkey's name was not untypical of the irrepressible, slightly school-boyish sense of humour of a man who called his horses Bryant and May (because they were "a perfect

One of R. Norman Shaw's own designs for the great mansion of Grim's Dyke, Harrow Weald. It shows the original front entrance.

Gilbert's library at Grim's Dyke is the background for this cartoon likeness drawn for the Daily Mirror in January 1904.

match"), and once wrote a mock-serious complaint to neighbour Thomas Blackwell about a straying dog that included the phrase "Please keep your Pickles out of my preserves."

Only in court, where he served as a local magistrate for many years, did he have to rein in his humour. Nevertheless when a wealthy young motorist claimed to be above the current laws on speeding, Gilbert reportedly fined him £5 with the wounding aside that "Had you been a gentleman, I should have fined you £10."

In fact, Gilbert was himself a well-known early motorist with a collection of fine cars in his specially converted stables including both a Rolls Royce and a Cadillac.

By the time of his move to Harrow Weald, Gilbert's working relationship with Sir Arthur Sullivan was somewhat strained (there was to be only one more collaboration, the less-than-successful *Utopia Ltd*) and Sullivan is believed to have made only one visit to Grim's Dyke.

A few notable exceptions apart, Gilbert seems to have lacked men friends in his later days but, then, men may not have taken kindly to the fact that he had extended the tennis court in his garden well beyond the regulation length to allow for the fact that he was both a big man (6ft 4ins), and a big hitter.

In addition to tennis, Grim's Dyke could also offer the attractions of a lake some 170 yards by 50 yards, which its owner had helped to dig out. Here, he swam regularly and here he was to meet his death – in circumstances that still retain an element of mystery.

On a Monday afternoon towards the end of May 1911, Gilbert, who was 74, drove to Harrow station to collect two young women he had promised to take swimming in the lake.

One was Winifred Emery, niece by marriage to the actor-manager Cyril Maude, to whom Gilbert had sold his London house before moving to Grim's Dyke. Miss Emery was then running a little school called Burnside in one of the houses recently built in Welldon Crescent and she brought with her a 17-year-old apprentice teacher, then known as Ruby Preece.

On arrival at Grim's Dyke, the girls apparently entered the water first but Ruby quickly got into difficulties. Gilbert immediately went to her rescue but, while she was holding on to his shoulders, as instructed, he suddenly sank from view. Taken from the water by members of his gardening staff, Gilbert was found to be dead.

No post mortem was ever done and at an inquest held in the Billiard Room of Grim's Dyke a few days later the jury returned a verdict of Accidental Death after hearing a doctor say he had no doubt death was due to "syncope of the heart" (basically a fainting fit) resulting from over-exertion.

After the expectedly lavish funeral, at which over 300 wreaths were received, Gilbert's ashes were finally laid to rest in a tomb at St. John's, Stanmore. Subsequently, a memorial was placed in the parish church of All Saints, Harrow Weald.

Lady Gilbert lived on at Grim's Dyke with Nancy, their adopted daughter, until her own death in 1936 but the bathing lake was closed off and partially drained.

An interesting footnote to the story is provided by the subsequent – and remarkably

The lake at Grim's Dyke much as it looked in May, 1911, when Sir William died attempting to rescue a young girl swimmer.

A typically Victorian gravestone marks Sir William's burial spot at St. John's, Stanmore. A plaque was also placed in All Saints, Harrow Weald.

Frederick Goodall, the popular Academician, for whom Grim's Dyke was first designed in the early 1870s.

Picturesque Egyptian scenes like this brought fame – and fortune – to Frederick Goodall.

The south front of Bentley Priory, for centuries one of the great houses of Middlesex.

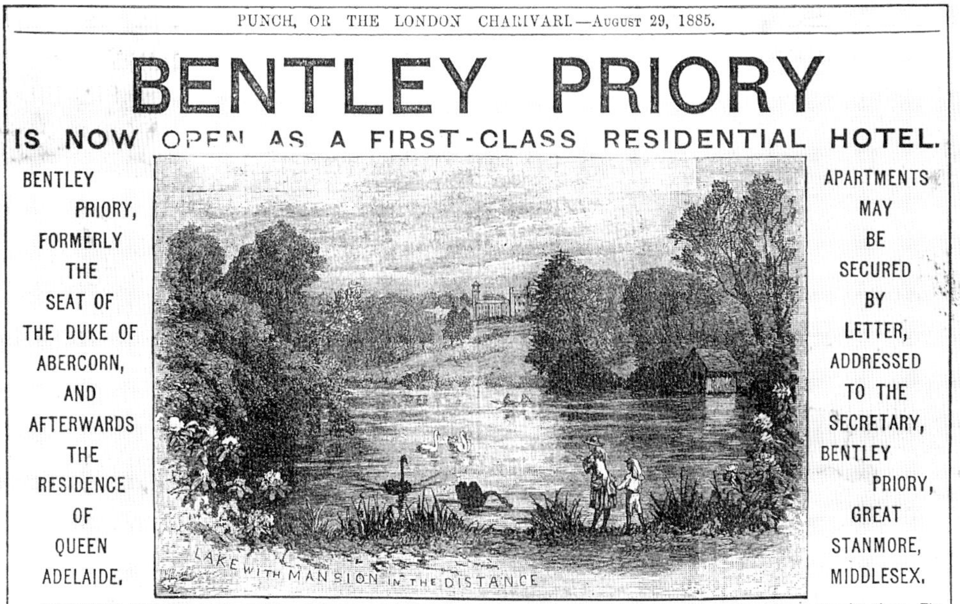

PUNCH, OR THE LONDON CHARIVARI.—August 29, 1885.

BENTLEY PRIORY

IS NOW OPEN AS A FIRST-CLASS RESIDENTIAL HOTEL.

BENTLEY PRIORY, FORMERLY THE SEAT OF THE DUKE OF ABERCORN, AND AFTERWARDS THE RESIDENCE OF QUEEN ADELAIDE.

APARTMENTS MAY BE SECURED BY LETTER, ADDRESSED TO THE SECRETARY, BENTLEY PRIORY, GREAT STANMORE, MIDDLESEX.

BENTLEY PRIORY, in the Parishes of Stanmore and Harrow, occupies a most delightful position and commands very extensive views. The Deer Park, Cedar Gardens, Terraces, and Ornamental Grounds cover 250 acres. Visitors have all the comforts and beautiful surroundings of an Old English Mansion at Moderate Hotel Charges. The distance from London is a little over ten miles by a good carriage road, and there is a capital service of Trains from Broad Street and Euston to Harrow. Carriages or Private Omnibuses from the Hotel may be ordered for any train.

A well-appointed Coach leaves the Métropole and Grand Hotels every morning (Sundays excepted), returning in good time in the evening.

An advertisement for Gordon's "First Class Residential Hotel" as it appeared in Punch magazine in August 1885.

Queen Adelaide, wife of King William IV, the only Queen to live – and die – in the borough.

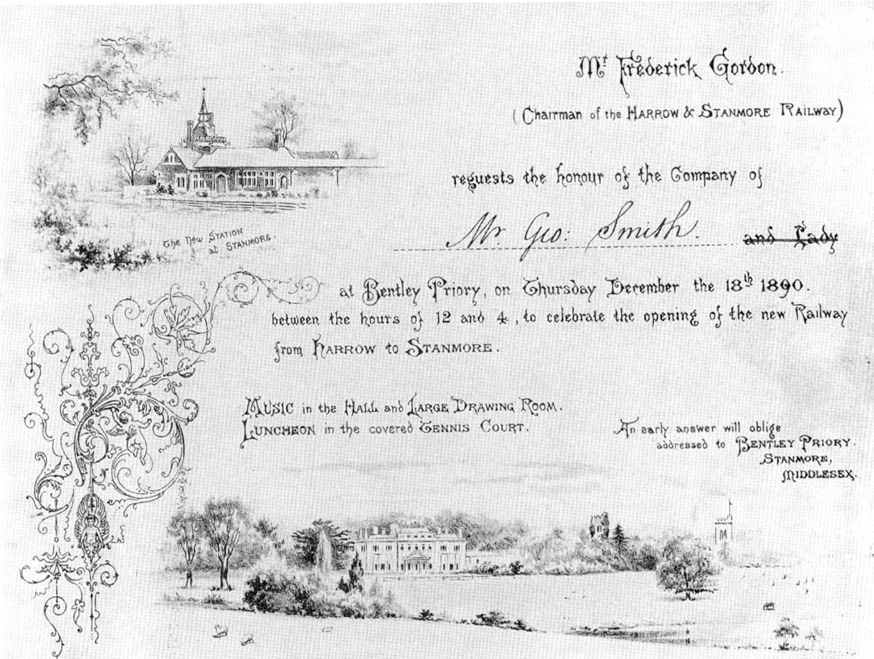

One of Frederick Gordon's lavishly illustrated invitations to the opening of the new Stanmore line in December, 1890. The pictures include (top left) the newly built station.

guests out-of-town, Gordon now decided to provide a railway for them and personally found most of the finance to lay a branch line running from the London and North Western Railway Station at Harrow & Wealdstone to a newly-built station in Stanmore. He also laid out a road – now appropriately called Gordon Avenue – across his grounds to the station.

Although the line opened with great celebrations at Bentley Priory in December 1890, earning a full page of illustrations in the *Daily Graphic*, the hotel project was not the expected success and Gordon, who had eleven children by two marriages, subsequently used the Priory as his private residence. As older residents will recall, the railway line continued to service the area for a further 70 years and the station, much altered, became a private house.

When, after some years as a girls' school, Bentley Priory was purchased by the Air Ministry in 1925, it was assumed that its glory days were at an end. In fact, this was only a new beginning for, in 1936, it became the Headquarters of Fighter Command and (as described in Chapter 36) the war-time salvation of the whole of Britain.

Stanmore station as it looks today, following its conversion – minus spire – to a private residence.

28. Three Remarkable Women

When the Woodridings estate of handsome semi-detached villas went up in Uxbridge Road, Hatch End, in 1855, the estate agent's prospectus made much of the generous size of the dining room, drawing room and five bedrooms. The kitchen, however, rated only the most cursory of mentions.

Yet one of those kitchens – at No.2 Chandos Villas – was the birthplace of many of the delicious recipes that brought lasting fame to their creator, Mrs Beeton.

The fact that she lived not in baronial splendour but in suburban comfort is just one of many surprises about this altogether remarkable lady. Another is her extreme youth since she was a mere 25 when her definitive *Book of Household Management* first appeared.

Some latter-day commentators – fellow cook Fanny Craddock among them – have suggested that Isabella Beeton would have been far too busy, bringing up her three children, to have written a volume of no fewer than 1112 pages.

Yet in assessing the work that bears her name, one should never underestimate the driving ambition of her publisher husband, Sam. It was Sam who first found the house in Hatch End to which he brought Isabella as a bride, following a somewhat unconventional wedding on Epsom racecourse. (Apparently her stepfather ran the grandstand!)

It was Sam, too, who was quick to spot the commercial potential of her recipes, publishing them first as supplements to his *Englishwomen's Domestic Magazine*. Even he, however, must have been amazed at the immediate success (60,000 copies sold in the first year) of what we would now call the hard-back edition.

For all her comparative youth, Mrs Beeton was not above admonishing as well as instructing her readers, pronouncing that there was no more fruitful source of family discontent than "a housewife's badly cooked dinners and untidy ways". Yet even the most hardened feminist could scarcely disagree with the assertion that "the more sunlight that comes into a home, the healthier the habitation".

With its large windows and spacious rooms, the Hatch End house obviously scored highly in this respect but Isabella was far from robust. For all the conventional view of her as a majestic Victorian matron, she actually died at 29, giving birth to a fourth child.

The Hatch End home, however, survived until the 1930s. At the time of writing the site is occupied by a restaurant where the Harrow Heritage Trust has recently erected a plaque in Isabella's memory.

Her name is also recalled by the nearby Beeton Close. Aptly enough, it backs on to the railway line that first brought the Beetons to Harrow and which Sam (sometimes in the company of his wife) used every working day throughout their Hatch End years.

Pinner, too, was now becoming an increasingly popular place to live. As such it clearly

Left *In life Isabella Beeton was far different from the mature Victorian matron of popular image.*
Right *Brought up at St. Mary's Vicarage, Annie Besant devoted much of her long life to championing women's rights.*

Marriage portrait of Horatia Nelson Ward, Pinner-based daughter of Lord Nelson.

recommended itself to a young man called Nelson Ward as a suitable home for his recently widowed mother. Although her married name was Mrs Philip Ward, mother's parentage could hardly have been more illustrious.

As the son's name suggests, Mrs Ward's father was England's great national hero, Horatio, Lord Nelson. Her mother, it is now generally accepted, was the equally famous (some would say notorious) Emma, Lady Hamilton, wife of Nelson's long-standing friend, Sir William Hamilton, whom Nelson never married. Yet, at the time, both mother and daughter did their level best to deny their relationship.

Nelson himself merely contributed to the mystery. Although, in his celebrated dying words, he apparently left Emma to the generosity of the nation, on the day of his death he also wrote in his pocket-book that he left "to the beneficence of my country, my adopted daughter, Horatia Nelson Thompson".

Given the circumstances of her childhood, one can understand Horatia's joy at making an early and happy marriage to a country curate and becoming, legitimately, Mrs Philip Ward.

The Reverend Ward later became Vicar of Tenderden, Kent, and Horatia seems to have been the ideal vicar's wife until his sudden death in 1839. Having recently suffered the additional loss of a daughter, Mrs Ward was especially grateful to accept the invitation of her son, Nelson, to join him in Pinner, where he was then living in West House in West End Lane.

Subsequently, Mrs Ward moved to New House (now rechristened Elmdene) in Church Lane and, later still, to a villa on the very same Woodridings estate that had been home to Sam and Isabella Beeton.

Just how secure her identity as Mrs Philip Ward had become was clearly demonstrated when another – and newsworthy – tragedy befell the family.

On a summer Saturday in 1872, Ellen, a grown-up daughter still living at home, was walking down Pinner High Street when she was knocked down and trampled by a bolting carthorse. Taken into the Queen's Head, she was immediately pronounced dead.

Such an event inevitably found its way into the columns of the local press but no connection was made with the Nelson family although the victim was, of course, the great hero's granddaughter.

When Horatia Ward herself died at 80 in March 1881, she was buried in the Paines Lane cemetery, Pinner. Here her tombstone proudly proclaims her as "the beloved daughter of Vice Admiral Lord Nelson". But visitors will look in vain for any mention of her mother.

In terms of her (often forgotten) achievements, a third Victorian woman, Annie Besant, deserves inclusion in our narrative although, in all honesty, Harrow failed to claim her much beyond adolescence.

Annie Wood, as she then was, came to Harrow in her ninth year when her widowed mother, Mrs Wood, took lodgings in the town so that her two sons could be enrolled as foundationers at Harrow School. Then, Mrs Wood hit on an even better money-making device. She would move into a house sufficiently large for her to offer board and lodgings to a num-

The Queen's Head in High Street, Pinner, around the time Ellen Ward was tragically killed.

Elmdene (centre) in Church Lane, photographed c.1892, was the Pinner home of Lord Nelson's descendants.

ber of Harrow pupils.

The then empty St. Mary's Vicarage on Church Hill proved the ideal location and the Head Master of the day, Charles Vaughan, ultimately agreed to her plan, providing that she also took under her roof a male house tutor.

Thus, Annie grew up in a largely boy's world, a circumstance which may well have shaped the wholly unconventional career she followed.

Although something of a tomboy, Annie was a gifted pianist and a frequent performer at the musical evenings, which were then a great feature of the Harrow social scene. At one of these gatherings, it seems likely she first met Miss Ellen Marryat, sister of the Captain Marryat, whose popular adventure stories such as *Midshipman Easy* and *Children of the New Forest* are, to this day, regularly adapted for television. Much taken with Annie, Miss Marryat invited her to become a companion to her niece, which necessitated a move to Dorset.

This was to be but the first of Annie's many exciting journeys. Married at 20 to a clergyman, Frank Besant, considerably older than herself, she later became involved with a self-proclaimed atheist, Charles Bradlaugh, and, with him, founded the Free Thought Publishing Company.

True to its name, the company brought out a volume daring to advocate birth control and both Bradlaugh and Annie Besant were brought to trial, accused of "depraving public morals". Although the two defendants won their case, the action had a tragic outcome for Annie, the Reverend Besant claiming and winning custody of their children.

At a time when the pioneering trades union movement was concerned almost exclusively with male labour, it was left to Annie Besant and like minded colleagues to champion the cause of the cruelly used women employees of the wealthy match company, Bryant and May, resulting in the famous – and successful – Match Girls' Strike.

Later, Annie Besant was converted to the Hindu-inspired doctrines of the Russian-born theosophist Helena Blavatsky and championed the cause of theosophy throughout her travels which took her both to America and to India.

The politics of the latter country were to become her consuming passion and, in 1916, she founded the Indian Home Rule League. A year later, she became the first Chairman of the Indian National Congress.

Annie Besant died in Madras in 1933 but it is claimed that she always kept a place in her heart for Harrow. Certainly, in her autobiography, she speaks lovingly of the old vicarage garden and of a trap-door in its fence "which swung open and displayed one of the finest views in England" – the view still to be enjoyed from the present terrace of St. Mary's.

Holy Trinity, Wealdstone, as it looked c.1909 when the Mothers' Union set off on their annual outing.

Crowds gather in 1849 to watch Lord Aberdeen lay the foundation stone of the present St. John's, Stanmore.

29. Spreading the Word

Where once the religious needs of Harrow's people were met wholly by the three historic churches of Harrow, Pinner and Stanmore, the last 150 years or so have witnessed the establishment of so many churches, chapels and missions – and, indeed, of so many different faiths – that any comment in a book of general interest must largely be confined to Harrow itself and thus rather more cursory than its writer would wish.

Inevitably, the greatest of changes has occurred in the once-vast parish of St. Mary's, Harrow on the Hill, which for much of its existence drew worshippers from as far afield as Wembley, on one side of the Hill, and Harrow Weald on the other.

As early as 1815, the St. Mary's vestry had bowed to the inevitable by allowing a small wooden chapel to be erected in Harrow Weald which later became the church of All Saints with the able Rev. Edward Monro as its first perpetual curate. In 1846, Monro also found time to establish a small college to train boys for the clerical and teaching professions. Although this failed to survive its founder's departure for Leeds, its existence is still acknowledged in the naming of Harrow Weald's College Hill Road.

On the other side of the Hill, Anne and Frances Copland gave some of the land they had inherited on the Sudbury Lodge estate for a church that became the present St. John the Evangelist, Wembley, built in 1846 to designs by Gilbert Scott.

The same busy architect's office also produced the designs for Christ Church, which arose on Roxeth Hill in 1862, just a year after the death of Vicar Cunningham. Cunningham, it was then discovered, believed that his memory might best be served by the building of another daughter church – this time in Greenhill – and St. John's, Greenhill, arose in 1866 to be followed in 1905 by today's much larger church.

Meanwhile, in Stanmore, around 1845, the existing parish church, consecrated by William Laud in 1632, was felt both to be too small for the growing district and possibly unsafe. So, in 1849, the foundation stone of the present, larger St. John's, was laid by the contemporary Rector's father, the Earl of Aberdeen, on a site adjoining the still-surviving 17th-century church.

The stone-laying ceremony was witnessed by the Dowager Queen Adelaide, widow of King William IV, who was then living at Bentley Priory. It was to prove her last public appearance before her death later that year.

The growth of Pinner, especially in the years following the opening of the Woodridings estate in 1855 (see Chapter 28), saw the building of a temporary church in Hatch End in 1865 for use as a chapel of ease to Pinner. This, in turn, led to the dedication of the present St. Anselm's, Hatch End, in 1895, named in honour of the Archbishop who had consecrated St. Mary's, Harrow, all those centuries before.

Not everyone, of course, held the established Church of England in quite the same high

Sunday in South Harrow in 1908,
as worshippers leave a Baptist Mission tent erected on the fields of Grange Farm.

A vanished Harrow landmark – the Methodist church in Bessborough Road shortly after its opening in 1904.

regard and history records the local growth of two distinct non-conformist groups – the Wesleyans and the Baptists – from the very earliest years of the 19th century.

The Wesleyans were, in fact, the first to acquire a permanent chapel on London (Roxeth) Hill in 1810, followed two years later by the Baptists who opened their own chapel in the present Byron Hill Road. The latter occasion was marked by a celebratory dinner at the King's Head Hotel attracting many guests who found it convenient to travel from Paddington to Alperton by canal boat. Sadly, the return journey was marred by a serious disturbance for which blame was clearly laid at the doors of Harrow School.

According to a contemporary Baptist church minute, "Nearly one hundred of the elder boys amused themselves by throwing large stones and mud at our friends...to the serious injury of several." To this day, no-one seems to be sure whether the boys were expressing their distaste for the new canal or the new dissenters or whether, at a time of notoriously lax discipline, they were just behaving badly.

Despite this less than encouraging start, the Baptists prospered in their new home and, in 1864, a more impressive chapel (which, as a factory, still survives) was built on the same site. Here Harrow's Baptists continued to worship until their move to College Road in 1908.

Their progress was much aided by the support of the Rev. Charles Hadden Spurgeon, one of the greatest Baptist speakers of the day, who in 1856 attracted a total of 1700 congregants to a one-day Baptist Mission held in the great barn of Grange Farm, Roxeth Corner. Spurgeon also attracted large crowds in 1863 when he gave a special address on behalf of the local building fund.

The Wesleyans, too, enjoyed a comparable success, enabling them to build a bigger chapel (now the Harrow Welsh Church) next to Middle Path, off Lower Road, before themselves moving to Bessborough Road in 1905.

Not for the first time, those of Roman faith faced rather sterner opposition and were thus required to wait longer for a proper meeting place of their own.

Sad to relate, even the idea of a Catholic church in our midst prompted someone describing himself as " a layman of the Church of England", to write to the *Harrow Gazette* in 1895 declaring that "such a prospect (should) stir up every Protestant...to see that it is through no neglect of his that any standing room is afforded to an alien faith".

Such prejudice, however, found a redoubtable opponent in the distinguished Catholic churchman, Cardinal Manning, who knew Harrow well, having been a pupil at its public school earlier that century.

In 1878 Manning invited to Harrow a group of Belgian nuns from the Third Order of St. Dominic's who took up residence at The Mount at the top of Sudbury Hill. Here they subsequently established St. Dominic's Convent School (now the borough's Catholic Sixth Form College).

With Manning's continued support, Harrow Hill next gained its first Catholic Mission, situated in little more than a corrugated iron hut in Roxborough Road. By 1894, however, support was such that a fine new church could be built. In the light of events related earlier in this narrative, its dedication could hardly have been more appropriate – the Church of Our Lady and St. Thomas of Canterbury.

Just after the turn of the century, a small group of German Fathers dedicated to St. Joseph – the Salvatorians – settled in Wealdstone where they, too, erected a little iron church, to which they added a companion building to serve as a parochial school.

They were later joined in their work by a communion of nuns, the Sisters of St. Chrétienne (otherwise known as St. Christiana). Together they sowed the seeds for the substantial education complex that now surrounds St. Joseph's church, Wealdstone, and which, for generations, has contributed so much to the well-being of young people from Harrow and beyond.

The Salvation Army also found the town of Harrow rather less than welcoming when, in 1886, they decided that there was work to be done in what many would have (mistakenly) regarded as a wholly prosperous district.

The *Harrow Gazette*, in particular, was horribly condescending in its reportage of the opening of what became an Army Citadel at Roxeth Corner, stating that both the morning and evening services were attended by "about 100 of the roughest element".

The columnist also felt obliged to add that "no unruliness marked the event".

The concerns of the local Board of Health were, at least, rooted in fact for the upper room in the original building could only be reached by an open step-ladder and the main meeting room itself was not only heated by a coal stove but also lit by ten small oil lamps.

Fortunately, no accidents occurred and, within 20 years, the money was found for the more impressive Citadel, which largely remains to this day.

30. The First Factories

Apart from isolated instances of brewing, brick-making and chalk-mining, industry plays very little part in the first 850 years of this narrative but, then, until the very end of the last century, Harrow was predominantly an agricultural community.

The brewers were the Stanmore Clutterbucks, who began brewing at the top of Stanmore Hill around 1763.

In the earliest days, at least, the Clutterbucks ran an essentially local operation with their own "tied" houses, including "The Vine" just yards away, and purpose-built cottages for their workers on the opposite side of the road to the brewery. For a while, too, they grew their own hops on the Warren House Estate.

By 1916, however, the company had ceased making its own beer and, seven years later, the current Clutterbuck sold the business to Cannon Breweries of Clerkenwell. In more recent times, much of the disused brewery building has been transformed into apartments although, happily, the clock tower and cupola, which had graced the premises for centuries, still survive.

Reports of brick-making in the district exist as early as 1589. Fourteen years later, the influential Gerards of Harrow Hill were accused by the neighbouring Pitt family of stealing 100 loads of sand with which to make bricks. To add insult to injury, the Gerards had then sold their "stolen" bricks at a price well below that which the Pitts normally charged!

Around 1830, a Charles Blackwell put the local bricks to especially good use by building a number of cottages for his brick-field workers at Old Redding, Harrow Weald.

Despite their modest scale, these cottages became widely known by the grandiose name "The City" – a rare example, according to the English Place Name Society, of a deliberate joke that just happened to stick. By the same token, the local hostelry (actually "The Case is Altered") was known to locals as "The Cathedral" on the very sound basis that every proper city must have a cathedral of its own!

Many names in the locality still provide evidence of the once flourishing brick trade, including the Kiln Nursery & Garden Centre. Similarly, the "clamp" of Clamp Hill harkens back to the trade term for any pile of bricks waiting to be fired.

The same Blackwell family also owned the extensive Pinner chalk mines, roughly below the present Montesole Playing Fields off Uxbridge Road. As pot-holers that have toured its still-navigable tunnels will testify, dates inscribed on the ceiling suggest that the mines were regularly worked for much of the 18th and 19th centuries.

Today, however, the Blackwell name is probably best known as one half of the famous Crosse and Blackwell brand of foodstuffs, whose story certainly merits a brief retelling.

Although the original firm was founded even earlier as Wyatt and West of Soho, the local

Horse and dray from Clutterbuck's Stanmore Brewery take voters to a 1906 election.

A rare 1908 photograph of Winsor & Newton's Bruce Road, Wealdstone, factory.

The imposing entrance to His Majesty's Stationery Office in Headstone Drive.

Women workers check chemical materials at Kodak c.1890.

connection was made as long ago as 1819 when Thomas Blackwell of the Harrow Weald family joined the company as an apprentice at virtually the same time as another 16-year-old called Edmund Crosse.

The two youngsters became firm friends and, some ten years later, determined to buy the company. Neither of their respective families initially approved of the idea but the lads were persuasive and, after the Blackwells had sold a farm at Bushey, the pair acquired the company for £600. It proved the best investment they could possibly make for, within a matter of years, most households would have on their shelves at least one of the ever-increasing number of Crosse and Blackwell products.

Meanwhile, in Harrow itself, manufacturing in the most modern sense of the word had to await the arrival of the railway; indeed, most of the companies initially attracted to the area found it convenient to base their operation as close to Harrow and Wealdstone station as possible.

Gunsmiths Cogswell and Harrison, in fact, came a little too close for safety and sparks from a passing steam engine caused a truly calamitous fire in 1894.

Yet it was Harrow's clear and unpolluted air, as much as its improved communications, that in 1890 prompted the American George Eastman, founder of the Kodak photographic company in Rochester, New York, to choose a smallish site in Wealdstone for his first overseas operation.

"Kodak" – a name invented by Eastman himself as one that could be easily pronounced anywhere in the world – prospered in its new setting and the original seven acres were soon extended almost ten-fold.

From the very first, Kodak offered a variety of jobs for women – all in relatively light and airy surroundings – and female staff quickly deserted less congenial companies. For example, employees of the Harrow School Laundry in Alma Road, South Harrow, willingly walked the few miles across the fields from Roxeth to Wealdstone for better conditions and, undoubtedly, better pay. Within a few decades in fact, the company had become the district's largest private employer with a workforce many thousands strong.

In the 1890s too, Headstone Drive acquired an elaborate printing works whose 170ft tall power-house chimney proudly proclaimed the name of David Allen & Sons.

If anything, this company proved too efficient for, when World War I broke out, the government decided to take it over for the production of all of the nation's wartime print, from ration books to posters.

Even though the company later won a considerable sum in compensation from the Old Harrovian Stanley Baldwin, then Financial Secretary to the Treasury, their links with officialdom remained strong and, in 1920, David Allen & Sons officially became His Majesty's Stationery Office.

Other notable arrivals in Wealdstone were Winsor & Newton, the suppliers of artists' materials, Hamilton's Brush Works and, from 1923, Whitefriars Glass Works, one of the most famous of its kind in the country.

Though far less of a household name (perhaps because their business was in coffins), Messrs. Ingall, Parsons, Clive and Company operated successfully in Masons Avenue from 1900-1939 while, from Stuart Avenue, Miss E.B. Jayne ran her flourishing Little Laundry Company.

Though the laundry continued to grow in size and reputation (and was ultimately taken over by the giant Allied Laundries), Miss Jayne persisted in using the original name and the original slogan – "Little But Good".

Later, during World War I, her management skills received unique recognition from Lloyd George, then Minister of Munitions, who gave her the task of recruiting and controlling the vast army of women required to work in munitions.

The brick-making kiln at Harrow Weald pre-1938.

The narrow ridge of Harrow Hill c.1890 prompted businesses to move downhill.

Just after World War I shops and a cinema – the Broadway – lined this busy stretch of Station Road.

31. The Growth of Greenhill

Hard as it may be to believe, less than 150 years ago, bustling Central Harrow was the tiny hamlet of Greenhill.

As such, it had around 150 inhabitants engaged – as surviving names such as Sheepcote Road suggest – in essentially rural pursuits. The junction of Sheepcote Road and Greenhill Lane (later Station Road) was, in fact, the heart of a little community which boasted a Manor House and Grange with, across the road, an old smithy, an 18th-century inn (the Six Bells, later the Marquis of Granby) and a village pond.

Yet such were the physical limitations of the then-existing township of Harrow on the Hill that the development of Greenhill was wholly unavoidable and, once it had begun, surprisingly rapid.

For a start, the Hill's many businesses and services, perched as they were on a narrow ridge, had no room at all for expansion – except down the hill. Similarly, a hill – and a steep one at that – was no kind of venue for the additional railway link with London, which everyone earnestly desired. (Harrow & Wealdstone station was, after all, a good mile or so away.)

So, when the new Metropolitan extension from Baker Street finally pushed its way out to Harrow in 1880, its station was built in the very heart of Greenhill on land that had once formed part of the Lowlands Estate, owned by the influential Rotch family.

Nevertheless the Hill, at that time, was still important enough for the original station name of Harrow to be changed to the palpably absurd name it bears to this day – Harrow on the Hill.

The Hill's prestige was also such that the original station, built in a reassuringly old-fashioned "Queen Anne" style, had its primary entrance on the Hill side where, right up until the 1920s, horse-drawn cabs would wait to drive wealthy passengers to their hill-top residences.

Situated as it now was between two stations, Greenhill could hardly fail to grow and the few original shops and businesses were quickly joined by others. Moreover, as recorded in Chapter 29, Greenhill was one of the first parts of the vast St. Mary's Parish to erect its own church – as early as 1866.

Though the Hill retained its own fire station until the 1960s – and its own bank until the 1990s – a great many other concerns had moved downhill to survive.

Among them was Harrow's very own building society, the Cunningham Permanent Building Society, begun in London Road by John William Cunningham, son of Harrow's famous Victorian vicar, which re-opened in Bessborough Road, and the principal Harrow Post Office which exchanged its relatively tiny premises in the High Street for a more commodious building (subsequently further enlarged) in College Road.

Indeed, when the *Harrow Observer* commented on "the tendency of businesses to migrate

Opening of a Metropolitan Line station in 1880 put Greenhill on the map.

The red-brick bulk of Harrow Technical College (left) dominates this 1920s view of Station Road.

from the scholastic heights to the low grounds", they knew exactly what they were writing about for, until its merger with the *Observer*, the earlier *Harrow Gazette* had itself been printed on the Hill.

Shopkeepers, too, such as John Wright Cooper, saw Greenhill as their promised land. Originally a baker and confectioner in the old Harrow High Street, Wright Cooper was among the first retailers to move into the newly built Greenhill Parade in Station Road where the family subsequently established the town's most successful suite of dining rooms known as the Gayton Rooms.

Other early Greenhill retailers were S.W. Hunt and R.B. Kennard, trading as timber merchants as early as 1884; the even better-known Thomas Lilley and William Skinner who opened Greenhill's first shoe shop early this century on land which they already owned in Station Road; and David Wynter, whose Greenhill Laundry, opened in 1898, quickly became one of Greenhill's biggest employers.

Less fortunate perhaps was W.H. Soper who, falling victim to the 1917 influenza epidemic (see Chapter 33), failed to witness the ultimate success of the town's very first department store, Sopers (now Debenhams), which he had the misfortune to open only months before the outbreak of World War I.

To the largely male list of entrepreneurs should be added at least one female name, that of Marion Hewlett. A daughter of the Harrow School doctor, Thomas Hewlett, Marion made it her life's work to ensure that a largely uneducated younger generation, working in service or in shops, should receive the benefit of "further education".

Starting with classes on technical subjects, such as carpentry and cooking, held in the Hill homes of her friends, she later established a small school at 100 High Street. This proved so popular that it quickly paved the way for Greenhill's first Technical School, opened in Station Road in 1903.

As older residents will recall, it survived there for well over 60 years, before moving to Watford Road where it gained important new premises and, ultimately, an important new status as the University of Westminster.

Isabella Rotch, who continued to live at Lowlands for some 55 years after the death of her barrister husband, might also be said to have had a dream about education – but, in her case, it was a recurring dream which, in very old age, she frequently recounted to the visiting Edgar Stogdon, then Vicar of Harrow.

In this dream, she claimed to see Lowlands invaded by hordes of young girls, all identically clad – a story that would scarcely be worth the retelling were it not for the fact that, within five years of her death in 1909, her property became the nucleus of Harrow Girls' County School, now absorbed into the Greenhill College complex. (By then, the Boys' County School in Sheepcote Road had been in existence for some three years as the first state-aided secondary school in the district.)

With Harrow School on the Hill effectively closed to local boys and the Lower School

Greenhill School in St. Ann's Road was already at least 40 years old when this turn-of-the-century picture was taken.

Greenhill acquired its own church in 1866, replaced some 40 years later by the present St. John's, seen here c.1908.

of John Lyon (see Chapter 23) having only a limited entry – and neither of them taking girls – Greenhill soon became home to many other schools.

There had, of course, been a highly regarded "village" school – subsequently Greenhill School in St. Ann's Road – from around 1859 but there was obviously still an opening for private schools, which now began to open in larger, suitably converted, houses.

In 1901, a school once run at The Firs in Byron Hill Road moved down to College Road to become the well-known Heathfield School, still very much alive and well in nearby Pinner. Similarly, two years later, The Crofts, near the village centre, was acquired for another notable survivor, now Peterborough and St. Margaret's School in Harrow Weald.

Soon, there was an equally rich choice of boys' schools, among them Cave's School (which became an earlier Harrow High School), in Sheepcote Road and Alpha School, Buckingham College and Quainton Hall, still remaining in Hindes Road where they began.

South Harrow station shown shortly after its 1903 opening.

Arnold Mitchell's "perfect cottage hospital" on Roxeth Hill first opened in 1906.

32. The Lull before the Storm

In books and plays and films the first thirteen years of the twentieth century are invariably portrayed as some kind of "Golden Age". And so, indeed, they were for the vast majority of Harrow's residents.

The fast-expanding middle classes, in particular, enjoyed the benefits of wider jobs opportunities, improved means of transport, more comfortable homes, better schools, hospitals and shops, even new and exciting forms of entertainment

Significant buildings new to the district included a station, off Roxeth's Northolt Road, on the newly electrified District Line. Opened in 1903, it not only brought the shopping emporiums of Kensington and the West End closer than ever before, it also prompted substantial residential development in the immediate station area. The only drawback, it seems, was the railway's somewhat arbitrary choice of a name for the station, South Harrow, which struck a blow against the older, much-loved district name of Roxeth, a blow from which the area never really recovered.

Three years later, Roxeth Hill – and the town – acquired a beautiful new hospital to designs by the gifted local architect, Arnold Mitchell. Regarded in its day as one of the most perfect cottage hospitals in England, it has recently lost the last of its patients and now awaits conversion for residential use.

Mitchell – and his near-contemporary Edward Schroder Prior – were to be responsible for many of the finest new buildings of this period. It is to Mitchell, for example, that we still owe the attractive Victorian ambience of Grove Hill and its environs for, having built Grove Hill Cottage (now White Tops) as his private residence in 1892, he set about surrounding himself with similar properties both in Grove Hill and the parallel Peterborough Road.

Prior, son of the redoubtable Hebe Prior who founded the still-extant Roxeth Mead School in 1855, also worked on a variety of public and private commissions, including the Red House and Lyon Villas in Middle Road, St. Mary's Mission House in West Street and Harrow School's Music Schools in Football Lane.

It fell to Mitchell, however, to design a new school building in South Hill Avenue named after the novel *Orley Farm*.

How it got this name could, in itself, be the matter for a novel.

The school actually began in a house on Sudbury Hill but, later, its owner E.M. "Teddy" Hastings, moved part of it into the old Trollope family home on Julian Hill (see Chapter 17). Later still, on buying a copy of Anthony Trollope's newly published *Orley Farm*, he realised the value of the Trollope connection and persuaded the novelist to allow him to call his new school after the novel. Hastings, in fact, was even allowed to use the novel's frontispiece drawing by the noted John Millais on his school prospectus.

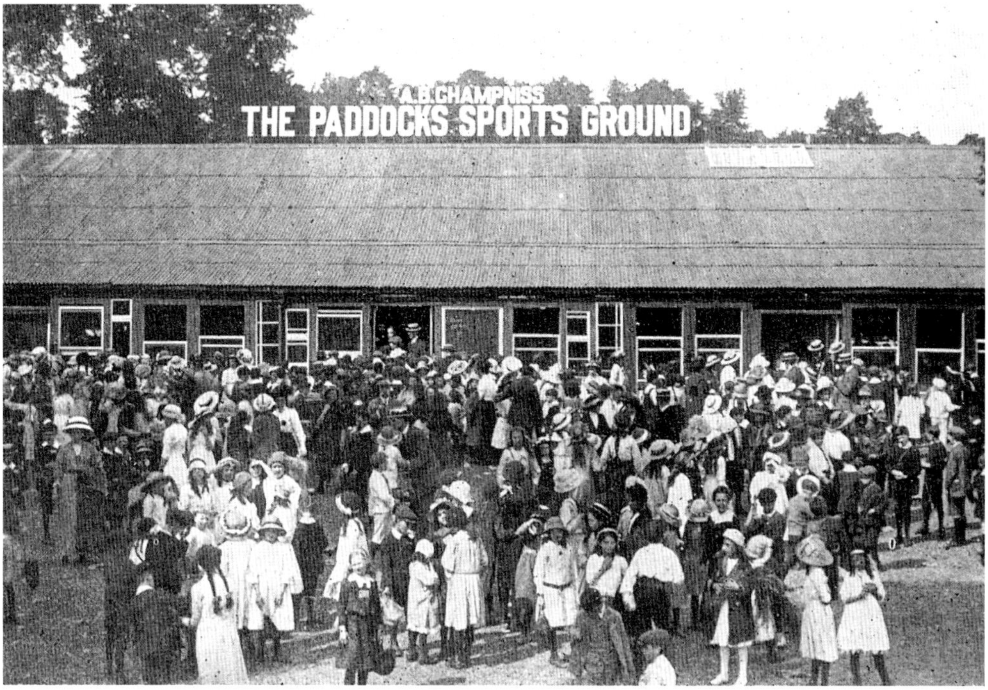

The Paddocks off Northolt Road was a favourite venue for family outings.

Crowds line Roxborough Bridge to watch the Olympic Marathon of 1908 routed through Harrow before ending at White City Stadium.

Around the same time, the fast-expanding Wealdstone acquired Bridge Schools situated on the Harrow side of the Wealdstone Railway Bridge to serve families from the many roads springing up on either side of Station Road.

Now linked to the Hill by way of Peterborough Road, Station Road itself (formerly Greenhill Lane) soon lost its purely residential character as numerous shops were built – often in the front gardens of existing properties, a fact that can still be deduced from their rooflines.

Many of these early retailers were destined to become household names, among them the grocers, Sainsbury's and Home & Colonial, and the shoe sellers, Freeman, Hardy & Willis.

In their bid for patronage, many shops offered home deliveries although, in these pre-motorised days, the companies invariably relied upon horse-drawn vans.

The motor car, in fact, was relatively slow to come upon the local scene: certainly, it was not until August 1898 that the local paper reported the passage of one such vehicle through the town.

The same *Harrow Gazette* also identified Dr. Lionel Ford, Head Master of Harrow, and the librettist, Sir William Gilbert, then living at Grim's Dyke (see Chapter 26) as early motoring enthusiasts.

Sadly, the first fatal accident anywhere in the country involving a petrol-driven car actually occurred in our midst in 1899. The victims were the driver and one of the passengers of a Daimler Wagonette which broke a back wheel while attempting to brake on the exceptionally steep Grove Hill. Ironically, the vehicle was on a test delivery run organised by the carriage department of London's Army & Navy Stores.

A few years later, Harrow made happier headlines in the rather unexpected context of the 1908 Olympic Games.

Since these were being staged in the built-for-the-purpose White City Stadium, it was decided to begin the marathon in Windsor and to route it through Harrow where a considerable crowd lined every pavement and every window along the way.

Not surprisingly, the event gave a healthy boost to local athletics and, within months, the *Harrow Observer* was staging its own marathon (though, in fact, the distance was considerably shorter), beginning and ending in the relatively new Harrow Recreation Ground in Pinner Road.

Local "entertainment" in these years was remarkably varied. For the intellectual elite, there was the Harrow Fifty Club, founded by winter sports pioneer and Harrow resident Sir Henry Lunn, which met every Saturday evening to discuss important contemporary topics.

With the help of hindsight, one particularly notes "The Recreational Needs of the Working Classes in Harrow", "The Pernicious Influence of Modern Journalism" and, especially in view of its 1913 date, "The Insufficiency of the Defensive Forces of The Crown".

Meanwhile those in search of more physical stimulus could find it in various pleasure gardens, such as The Paddocks off Northolt Road, a 30-acre park on which farmer A.B. Champniss had sited virtually every kind of contemporary amusement, from swings to roundabouts, from donkey rides to a miniature railway track. Able to accommodate – and feed – up to 2500 visitors at a time, The Paddocks became one of the most popular locations for school, church and family outings in the whole of Middlesex.

There were also many acres of pleasure grounds, known as Wembley Park, at the foot of the so-called Watkin's Folly, a tower intended to rival the Eiffel Tower in Paris. Unfortunately, this brainchild of Sir Edward Watkin, one-time chairman of the Metropolitan Railway Company, failed (almost literally) to get off the ground.

The scheme began well enough. Over 60 international designers responded to his invitation to create a tower of some 1200ft (some 200ft taller than the original) and, once a design had been accepted, Watkins put in a railway station at Wembley Park to transport the anticipated crowds.

Yet a combination of bad planning, uncongenial clay soil and, above all, shortage of capital saw the project come to a halt after the first 160ft platform had been built.

Watkin's later hopes that it might become "a Marconi Station" were also dashed and, after a limited period as the focal point of the Wembley Park pleasure grounds, the incomplete tower was demolished by explosives in 1907.

Watkin's choice of site, however, was a good one for, had his tower been completed, it would have arisen precisely where Wembley Stadium stands today.

For all that it is virtually obligatory to applaud the Edwardians for the richness of their home-made amusements, it has to be said that Harrow residents were remarkably quick to welcome the first cheap mass-produced alternative.

This was, of course, the moving picture which, prior to 1910, any travelling showman could project in any convenient hall, wholly without licence. For this reason alone, it is hard to tell precisely where and when the first local film performance took place but it seems likely to have been in Wealdstone where there was a ready-made audience from the nearby factories.

Certainly, both Rowley's Coliseum and Picture House in Masons Avenue and the Star Theatre in Byron Road are known to have been operating by 1909, a year before Harrow itself acquired the Empire and Picturedome. Despite a good site in a red-brick block at the junction of St. Ann's Road and Clarendon Road, the Picturedome ran into financial difficulties after just three years and was quickly converted for use as the still-remembered Adams Furniture Stores.

Early newsreels, which regularly recorded such royal events as Queen Victoria's funeral, undoubtedly helped to bring her son, Edward VII, even closer to his people although he was, in fact, by no means a stranger to Harrow.

As Prince of Wales, he had brought his wife (later Queen Alexandra) to Harrow School Speech Day in 1894 and, without her, he not infrequently visited Warren House at Stanmore, especially if the guest list included one of the current Royal Favourites.

It must have seemed impossible that this stable, ordered, somewhat complacent world could ever end. Yet, long before the first shots of World War I were fired, there came an event that proved that the unthinkable could actually occur.

On April 10, 1912, the White Star liner *Titanic* set sail on its maiden voyage to New York. Proclaimed unsinkable, not least because of the 16 water-tight compartments beneath the water-line, it nevertheless struck an iceberg on April 15 and promptly sank with the loss of more than 1500 lives.

Many intriguing disaster stories have since been told but few more fascinating than the circumstances surrounding the survival of Charles Williams, a world-class racquets player and racquets instructor at Harrow School, who lived in Drury Road.

Among its unprecedented facilities, the *Titanic* boasted a racquets court and Williams claimed to have just left the court for the smoking room when "he felt a slight shudder".

What happened next is more open to doubt. According to a statement he allegedly made on reaching New York, Williams had then jumped into the sea from a deck on the starboard side, spending some eight hours in – or possibly on – the water before being rescued. Yet evidence given by the ship's Fifth Officer at the official enquiry mentioned Williams by name as "a chap I took for rowing".

Naturally eager to celebrate the survival of a prominent member of staff, the Harrow School magazine the *Harrovian* wrote at some length about his escape. They, however, told a slightly different story in which Williams was "picked up by a raft on which he remained until the arrival of (the rescue ship) Carpathia".

The local paper, the *Harrow Gazette*, also sought an interview with Williams on his return to Harrow. Instead, they were obliged to report that "under medical evidence, it seemed advisable not to speak to him about the disaster". They did, however, secure a brief interview with his wife in which she claimed that "many mis-statements have been made in the newspapers concerning what Mr. Williams is supposed to have said in New York".

Did Williams change the details of his story simply because he was ashamed to admit that his peak physical condition had (quite sensibly) marked him out as someone capable of rowing other survivors to safety? At this late date, we shall presumably never know.

In any event, within a matter of months, Harrow's citizens – in common with most of the civilised world – had to contend with even more personal and pressing matters of survival.

Stanmore resident William Leefe Robinson who became a national hero by shooting down a German Zeppelin.

33. Harrow at War

At this remove, perhaps the most terrifying aspect of the outbreak of World War I is the breakneck speed with which so many of Harrow's young men were translated from a largely untroubled peace-time to the very worst that war could offer.

Within days of the declaration of war against Germany on August 4th 1914, a transit camp for regular soldiers was established at Halls Corner, Harrow Weald (where Fontwell Close stands today). Simultaneously, railway sleepers were being unloaded at the railway sidings in nearby Cecil Road and, by the 18th of the month, troops were already embarking for France from this makeshift platform.

Among them were men of the Seaforth Highlanders and the Royal Warwickshire Regiment whose C platoon was then commanded by the young Lieutenant Bernard Montgomery, destined to become, in a later conflict, the famous Lord Montgomery of Alamein.

Events moved equally swiftly for the local "terriers", the 9th Middlesex Battalion of the Territorial Army. Since they were away at their annual summer camp when war broke out, many members returned home for a few days only before enlisting for the duration.

Nowhere, however, are the cruel realities of these early days more vividly evoked than in consecutive issues of the Harrow School magazine, the *Harrovian*.

The fifth issue of the twenty-eighth volume dated July that year is filled with happy reminiscences of Speech Day and the Eton and Harrow match, while its correspondence columns tackle nothing more serious than the ideal ingredients for a "Strawberry Dringer", a summer confection much favoured on the Hill. Yet, by October 6th, when the sixth issue was published, most of its pages were taken up with lists of Old Harrovians already killed or wounded in battle.

"Yet the boys never faltered", says C.H.P. Mayo, a contemporary housemaster, "their only fear was lest it should be over before their time to go".

Mayo, as he wrote in his 1928 book of reminiscences, had no doubts that these young men deserved preferential treatment. "Supplies were often brought to us under the cover of the darkness of night", he recalled, "lest hungry people in the town should think that we were being too generously treated at their expense, not appreciating the fact that we had some 40 or 45 boys who, if the War lasted, would be required to officer the new armies."

If they could not as yet fight, Harrow School pupils found plenty of other ways to support the war effort, from turning school gardens into allotments to helping make shells in the school workshops (which were also used for toy-making by Belgian refugees).

The outbreak of hostilities inevitably put a halt to many projects designed to extend and improve the town. Captain E.G. Spencer Churchill, of the Northwick family, was obliged to

In the early days of World War I, thousands of regular soldiers marched through Wealdstone en route to their Harrow Weald transit camp. The Seaforth Highlanders pass the site where, less than a decade later, a war memorial was erected to their memory.

Men of the Warwickshire regiment pass the Coronet cinema, on the corner of Graham Road, Wealdstone.

abandon a particularly grandiose scheme for a miniature town of small houses on land he had called Northwick Park after his family estates on the Gloucester–Worcestershire borders. In fact, only three of the many planned roads were actually completed – Northwick Avenue, Rushout Avenue and Churchill Avenue, all, incidentally "family" names – and vast acres of the undeveloped site soon became a mobilisation site for the troops of the British 4th Division.

Pride in country as well as pride in manhood saw an early surge in recruitment with over a million men answering Lord Kitchener's call to arms before the end of 1915. In Harrow alone, in just one week, some 305 men enrolled for service at a special orderly room set up in a house in Grove Hill Road.

Similarly when members of two local companies of the national reserve were urged to volunteer for the Regular Army, 63 out of 65 men on parade are said to have stepped forward.

In this initial eagerness to enlist, the use of subterfuge was not unknown. Harry Wilkins' invaluable *Greenhill*, for example, tells the story of four teachers from Greenhill School who, wanting to serve together, were dismayed when the first failed his eyesight test. Nothing daunted, the other three committed the optician's chart to memory and passed the details to the failed applicant, who returned to the recruiting office, re-took the eye test – and passed!

Once the full horrors of trench warfare became more widely known, however, there was an inevitable decline in the number of volunteers and single men were soon required by law to register (or "attest") their willingness to serve. Although in January 1916, the *Harrow Observer* was able to report that about one thousand men had attested in the paper's area, the scheme generally failed to produce the large numbers required for a war calamitously high in casualties and, in March 1916, a Conscription Act for single men was enforced.

As a further boost to recruitment, local employers were now encouraged to make more use of the services of older men and "where conditions allow, women workers". (The first specific mention of women workers can be found in Harrow Council's minutes for March 1915.)

In any event, more civilians found themselves in the firing line than in any previous conflict. As early as December 1914, the Germans had made the first-ever air raid on British soil (at Dover) and, before the war's end, enemy attacks from both sea and air had killed over one thousand civilians and injured more than twice that number.

For many local residents, however, Zeppelin activity over London was more a source of spectacle than of anxiety and the local press was full of excited accounts of crowds gathering on higher ground (such as Peterborough Hill and the Wealdstone Railway Bridge) to watch the Zeppelins run the gauntlet of London's anti-airship barrage.

An October 1917 entry refers, somewhat artlessly, to "a wonderful air spectacle, the most wonderful that has ever been seen by residents", a later column commenting that many members of the large crowd remained watching until the early hours.

Meanwhile, East Enders (somewhat curiously described by the local Medical Officer of Health

Pupils of Wealdstone's Bridge Schools entertain war-wounded veterans on May Day, 1917.

The Rev. Geoffrey Woolley, winner of the first T.A. Victoria Cross, inspects the belfry during his subsequent ministry at St. Mary's Harrow.

as "aliens from London") were flocking to the district in search of hospitality – and safety.

German air activity also promoted Harrow Council to circulate local households with instructions on extinguishing unnecessary lights and, in a fascinating foretaste of World War II's total black-outs, to use only those rooms where windows were effectively screened.

By an interesting coincidence, the first enemy airship to be brought down on British soil – at Cuffley in Hertfordshire – actually fell to a man who had made his war-time home in Gordon Avenue, Stanmore.

He was, of course, William Leefe Robinson, who won the Victoria Cross for his exploits and in whose honour the present Harrow Weald public house is named.

Unhappily, Leefe Robinson did not live long enough to enjoy his new-found fame. Returning to duty in France, he was himself shot down and captured in Douai (currently the French town twinned with Harrow).

As a prisoner in Holzminden camp, Leefe Robinson seems to have run foul of its harsh commander, Niemeyer by name.

The British hero was, therefore, in a sorry physical condition by the time of his repatriation in December 1918 and, falling an easy prey to influenza, he died before the year was out.

His Stanmore-based sister insisted that he was the victim not of disease but of Niemeyer who, she said, "employed every instrument of cruelty against him".

One of the very first Victoria Crosses of the war, won at Mons, also went to a local man, Charles Edward Garforth who, only a matter of weeks before, had been an assistant in a shoe shop in St. Ann's Road. A former pupil of Greenhill School, he was suitably honoured by the local authorities who presented him with an illuminated scroll and other gifts.

Another hero, even better known locally, was Geoffrey Woolley to whom, at the age of 23, fell the honour of receiving the first Victoria Cross to be awarded to a Territorial Officer. Woolley, who added both a Military Cross and an OBE to his decorations, later entered the Church before becoming an assistant master at Harrow School.

Then, in 1944, after further service as an army chaplain, he returned to the Hill as vicar of St. Mary's, a post he held for the next eight years.

Other young officers were not so fortunate and Woolley's church was the recipient of an especially poignant double memorial to Geoffrey Welsford and Francis Whitworth Owen, both sons of Harrow masters. Friends since childhood, they were killed in action on two consecutive days in March 1916. One was 20, the other 21.

Sadly, thousands of animals were also recruited to the allied cause and a certain Major E.H. Richardson achieved a measure of fame by pioneering the training and provision of war dogs from his kennels on Grove Hill. By the end of the war, numerous battalions were able to pay tribute to the skills of "Richardson's dogs" in a variety of jobs from guard work and patrols to espionage hunts.

Harrow can also claim a further pioneer in the London Road-based psychiatrist, Dr. Hugh Crichton-Miller who was among the very first to tackle the traumas of shellshock.

Later, he was to put his experience to valuable peace-time use in setting up the clinic which, as Bowden House, survives on Harrow Hill.

Two Pinner-based humorists, Bert Thomas and William Heath Robinson, are also fondly remembered for the cartoons and satirical drawings that helped to keep the nation laughing. The phrase "Heath Robinson" is still used by many people to describe any kind of bodged or ill-made mechanical contraption, little realising that it originates with the specifically anti-German cartoons that Heath Robinson regularly drew for such popular magazines as the *Bystander* and the *Illustrated London News*. Heath Robinson, who lived first in Hatch End and, later, at Moy Lodge, Moss Lane, Pinner (which currently bears a GLC Blue Plaque in his memory), published many of his drawings in book form, often with jokey war-time titles such as *Hunlikely*.

Equally popular at the time were the cartoons of Bert Thomas who then lived at Devonshire Road, Hatch End. His celebrated drawing of an unhurried Tommy pausing to light up his pipe and captioned "Arf a Mo, Kaiser" raised a phenomenal £250,000 for a servicemen's tobacco fund.

Thomas continued drawing into his old age and, when living at Church Farm, Pinner, in World War II, produced another classic drawing. Known as "His Red Letter Day", it raised considerable sums for the Red Cross and St. John Prisoner of War Fund.

The so-called Great War finally came to an end on November 11, 1918 but, for many in Harrow, it was far from being the end of their suffering. Weakened by the privations of wartime, hundreds fell victim to the so-called "Spanish Flu", one of the most virulent worldwide influenza epidemics ever known.

Worst hit locally was the increasingly populous Wealdstone. Despite the shutting down of all elementary schools and the flushing of the streets with powerful disinfectants, entire households went down with the disease and the death toll quickly reached fifty.

Harrow itself inevitably had its share of the epidemic but not, as the Medical Officer of Health cheerfully reported "an unduly large share". Nevertheless, in actual figures, this still meant the death of some thirty residents, young and old. In addition, Harrow School lost two of its pupils and a nurse.

The guns that sounded to mark the official end of the war were everywhere welcomed with heartfelt relief and thanksgiving. Yet, given the epidemic's impact, they heralded a celebration far more muted than might otherwise have been expected.

34. Votes for Women

In requiring women to do a variety of jobs previously the sole preserve of their menfolk, World War I undoubtedly helped them towards their goal of equal voting rights. Yet the battle – a true battle in which lives were both lost and ruined – had begun many decades before: certainly, well before 1903, the year in which Mrs Emmeline Pankhurst founded the Women's Social and Political Union (the W. S.P.U.), the so-called "suffragette movement".

As early as 1874, in fact, the *Harrow Gazette* reported that the Harrow Public Hall was packed for a discussion on "the admission of women householders to the exercise of Parliamentary Franchise". Even in those distant days, the subject provoked considerable emotion and it seems that the speakers were frequently interrupted by what were described as "unaccountable and unwarrantable noises from the balcony".

In the event, the meeting ultimately resolved that the continued exclusion of women from Parliament was "injurious" although, as the *Gazette* somewhat wryly pointed out, ladies had "formed the larger part of the assembly".

Subsequent suffrage meetings in Harrow were increasingly stormy until, in 1913, one such gathering could only go ahead after the most elaborate precautions had been taken to preserve order. Nevertheless, despite subjecting all tickets to the closest scrutiny, securing all windows and having a strong force of police within call, the speakers were subjected to a whole series of indignities. Snuff and pepper were sprayed, the lights were frequently extinguished and, worst of all, "obnoxious chemical fumes arose from a tin placed beneath the seats". Those faint-hearted enough to flee the hall then had to run the gauntlet of a large cat-calling crowd.

Street corner speakers – and there were many – were even more vulnerable to abuse.

As recently as 1969, a Pinner veteran called Charles Paradine recalled being paid sixpence a week to collect rotten eggs and flour from local shops with which "the men of the village pelted the suffragettes".

On occasion, however, the hostility was much more frightening. After Mrs. Phyllis Verden had spoken in Pinner, it was reported that a mob of at least two hundred angry people marched to her home at Pinnercote, Paines Lane, and bombarded it with stones, breaking a dozen or more windows. In response, Mrs.Verden told the local press that, if physical violence was again offered to her, she would not hesitate to shoot to protect herself and her property.

Such mindless and churlish opposition merely strengthened the resolve of all good suffragettes, one of whom (Emily Davidson) set the whole world talking by throwing herself into the path of the King's horse during the 1913 Derby.

Harrow ladies also clearly demonstrated that they were willing to suffer – if not to die – for their cause. The first to be imprisoned was the very young Lily Sampson Mosen of St. Kilda's Road, Harrow, on a charge of demonstrating outside the House of Commons. Though prison

Right from its opening in 1891, Kodak Ltd were unusual in the number of jobs available to women workers.

Miss Jayne of The Little Laundry was personally chosen by Lloyd George to recruit and supervise women munitions workers in the 1914–18 War.

food at this time was notoriously inedible, Mrs Mosen's only complaint was that the vegetables were not properly cleaned. She even found amusement in the fact that she was obliged to wear over-sized prison shoes, which frequently came off during her exercise periods.

Janie Terrero of Rockstone House, Paines Lane, Pinner, who was secretary of the Pinner branch of the W.S.P.U., did not fare quite so well. One of hundreds of women who, with hammers hidden beneath their muffs, had made a concerted attack on shop windows in the West End, she was initially offered bail of £200. "I did not think I was worth so much", she wrote to her Argentinian-born husband. Instead, she chose to serve a 4-month sentence in Holloway where she went on hunger strike. In papers now held at the British Museum, she wrote, "I do not ask for any privilege or even for mercy but merely what seems to be the most difficult thing for an Englishwoman to obtain at the present time – and that's justice."

Yet Mrs Terrero had the consolation of knowing that, back home, her husband was assuring her supporters that, she would "continue the good work so satisfactorily carried on at Pinner".

Though she managed to stay out of prison, Esther Knowles, who subsequently lived at Francis Road, Harrow, was also actively involved in the conduct of the W.S.P.U. Originally the movement's youngest office girl, she later became personal private secretary to Lord Pethick-Lawrence, the union's treasurer and editor of the paper, *Votes For Women*.

Perhaps inevitably, the movement attracted its share of fanatics, and increasingly violent excesses, such as the planting of several bombs and the slashing of the Velasquez *Rokeby Venus* at the National Gallery, occasioned a considerable loss of public good will.

Soon what the Press dubbed "suffragette mania" was gripping the country. The Governors of Harrow School, for example, felt that, in the light of such outrages, it was no longer safe to keep John Lyon's original School Charter and Statutes at the Vaughan Library. Instead, they sought the greater security of the strong-room of the Hill's London and County Bank.

From a distance of some eighty years, it must be admitted that some of these anxieties were not without their funny side. In Pinner, a policeman, finding the parish church unlocked one night, decided to investigate. To his horror, he discovered pieces of the organ scattered all over the church, an "outrage" which he immediately attributed to a suffragette bomb. In fact, the organ had been deliberately dismantled by a specialist firm employed to carry out repairs.

The local historian E.M. Ware also tells how the ticket collector at Hatch End station heard a loud ticking sound coming from a parcel left under a platform seat. Since the parcel was marked "Votes For Women", he summoned the police who sensibly dropped it into a bucket of water. Only then were the parcel's contents revealed to be an alarm clock of the cheapest kind. Nobody owned up to the prank although it is said that the choirboys of St. Anselm's, Hatch End, came under suspicion!

The needs of war, however, did much to change previously entrenched attitudes and, in June 1917, the Commons voted to give the vote not, it has to be admitted, to all women, but to those over the age of 30. Sadly, it took a further eleven years before the Equal Franchise Bill allowed women over 21 equal voting rights with men.

In his role as MP, Oswald Mosley dedicates the Wealdstone war memorial on Armistice Day, 1923.

Two years earlier, Harrow residents dedicated their memorial on a Grove Hill site that once housed an animal pound.

35. The Years Between

Even the least historically aware of us must surely know that the period between the two World Wars was one of significant change and growth for Harrow; after all, the evidence is all around us in street after street of houses that transformed a number of previously isolated local communities into a single highly developed borough.

That there was a pressing need for much of this development was already apparent at the end of World War I when the Medical Officers of Health of both Wealdstone and Harrow, then separate administrative districts, spoke in their 1918 reports of a serious shortage of homes in their respective areas.

Of the two, Wealdstone was obviously the worst off, the M.O.H. reporting that some degree of over-crowding was already forcing many workers in the Wealdstone factories to live elsewhere. He added that the building of more factories, which he saw as a distinct "probability", would only aggravate the situation.

As it quickly proved, there would be no lack of builders – and local companies too – eager to take up the challenge. But, first, the town had a duty to remember its war dead and, one by one, virtually every community raised its own memorial.

Whilst Wealdstone chose a useful clock tower in the High Street, Harrow built a more conventional memorial on land given by Harrow School at the foot of Grove Hill, a site which had once been the town pound where straying farm animals were held until claimed.

The town's most elaborate memorial – a handsome block comprising several multi-purpose meeting rooms – was put up by Harrow School. Designed by Sir Herbert Baker, best known as the architect of the Bank of England, this new block effectively changed the look of the very top of the Hill for its construction required the removal of several old properties including Dame Armstrong's House and Church Hill House between the High Street and Church Hill. At the memorial's heart remains the notably poignant Alex Fitch Room, erected in memory of a 19-year-old lieutenant killed within days of the Armistice, who personifies the staggering 644 former pupils and staff – virtually a complete school roll – who were killed in the conflict.

Although, as we have seen, the town's own officers had already identified the need for more housing, much of the impetus for growth came from bodies outside Harrow, such as the Metropolitan Railway Company. Since they owned a vast expanse of land along the tracks they had laid from Baker Street to Rickmansworth, "the Met" now began to promote this land for building, for which purpose they coined a particularly emotive description – "Metroland".

"Metroland" was later to be immortalised by that most popular of poets, John Betjeman, many of whose verses mocked, in the most affectionate way imaginable, the railway's prom-

CUCKOO HILL ESTATE, PINNER

8 minutes' walk from Pinner Station (Metro.)

THE CITY MAN'S IDEAL RESIDENTIAL SUBURB

AN IDEAL TYPE ON THE ESTATE.

SUPERIOR FREEHOLD VILLAS AND SPACIOUS BUILDING PLOTS FOR SALE

Room for Garage. Houses built to your own ideas and designs. Government Guaranteed Title. Good Road. Main Drainage. Gas, Water, Electricity. Mortgages arranged. Expert advice on all matters. Good Schools. Tennis Courts are on the Estate. Inspection cordially invited.

Write for Brochure to **W. A. TELLING, LTD.**

CUCKOO HILL ESTATE OFFICE, STATION APPROACH, PINNER

TEL.: PINNER 598

EASTCOTE END PARK ESTATE :: EASTCOTE

(Close to Eastcote Station)

Attractive 3-Bedroom Houses and Bungalows. Write for full Particulars to :

W. A. TELLING, Ltd., Estate Office, Eastcote Stn. TEL.: PINNER 210

SAY YOU SAW IT IN "METRO-LAND."

Page 122

In this typical pre-war house advertisement from the publication "Metroland", Pinner is dubbed "The City Man's Ideal Residential Suburb".

Kenton Park Parade was so much a T. F. Nash creation that this picture was featured in the company's 1933 brochure.

ise to deliver "country life" conveniently close to London.

The subsequent choice of nearby Wembley, first for Wembley Stadium, opened in 1923, and the following year for the vast British Empire Exhibition, also helped to publicise the semi-rural attractions of an area which was, indeed, less than ten miles from Charing Cross.

The Exhibition – many of whose grand buildings still stand along today's Olympic Way – was a success beyond its organisers' dreams and, by the time it closed its doors in October 1925, it had registered a phenomenal 27,102,598 admissions.

Harrow was now firmly on the map – and, if anyone was going to keep it there, it was the remarkable T.F. Nash who, from a registered office in Eastcote Lane, South Harrow, built one of the biggest and most productive construction companies in the country.

At its peak, Nash was able to claim a totally integrated and essentially local operation embracing a vast joinery works at Wealdstone, a substantial heavy transport fleet, even spacious garages for the many luxury automobiles in which prospective buyers were whisked around his latest estates.

In Kenton alone, Nash built a veritable township comprising some 2200 houses and shops off the Kenton Road before turning his attention to the largely undeveloped Rayners Lane.

In 1933, the company's advertising brochure was able to announce that 1000 homes had been completed in that area and that a further 3500 houses, shops and other premises were in preparation. These ultimately included the one-time Grosvenor cinema, now considered the apogee of 1930s art deco design (and thus preserved from demolition).

A great believer in the power of publicity and promotions, Nash even staged a Grand Shopping Week in the mid 1930s when a triumphal arch was suspended across Alexandra Avenue, South Harrow and firework displays and other attractions staged for intending buyers.

Equally active in the transformation of the town were three other local companies: E.S. Reid, who developed the popular Harrow Garden Village, north of Rayners Lane station, Cutler & Sons who built extensively in and around Pinner Road and Frederick & Charles Costin whose company developed much of the south side of Kenton.

Laing Estates and Harry Neal were also familiar names on Harrow's For Sale boards. Neal's company was also involved in the somewhat curious circumstances by which the town finally gained the outdoor swimming pool it had been discussing for decades.

It seems that, after a council estate had arisen off Lascelles Avenue, the council found itself with left-over land in Charles Crescent which, it was agreed, should be dug out as a pool. Since there were no funds to cart away the tons of excavated earth, they were simply banked up around the pool's sides, fortuitously providing a landscaped setting that, together with an uninterrupted view of St. Mary's, quickly proved one of the pool's greatest assets.

Shortly after its opening, the pool was considered good enough to host a Swimming Gala in which the British Empire was challenged by the United States, captained by none other than the 1924 Olympic swimming champion, Johnny Weissmuller, later to become one's

The 240ft high Roxeth gasometer whose building provoked much local anger.

At the height of his success, builder T. F. Nash erected this triumphal arch across the present Alexandra Avenue, South Harrow.

favourite screen Tarzan.

The one real threat to all this activity might well have been the General Strike of May 1926, which was intended to bring the country to a complete halt by shutting down all manufacture, transport and communications. Instead, a vast civilian army arose to undertake all the essential jobs and the strike collapsed within ten days – although the bitterness lingered on, as the letters column of the local press clearly showed.

Whilst one lady correspondent wrote in praise of the politeness of the improvised rail staff which she found "in striking contrast to what one has experienced for some time past", another more thoughtful reader was appalled by the tone of a church parade, held at St. Peter's, West Harrow to celebrate the end of the strike.

"Anything less calculated to ensure peace and promote concord could not be conceived", he wrote.

The Old Harrovian premier of the day, Stanley Baldwin, received many plaudits for his handling of the situation, not least from his old school who wrote of their pride that "you, a son of Harrow, have known how to maintain the spirit of true charity in our midst whilst never compromising principle".

Although it is frequently (perhaps conveniently) forgotten, Baldwin was not the only political figure of the day with strong Harrow connections.

In 1918, Harrow's Conservative Member of Parliament – and at 22, the youngest Member at Westminster – was the charismatic but ever controversial Oswald Mosley.

Already highly individual in his views – and never backward in expressing them – Mosley quickly earned the disapproval of the leading local paper, the *Harrow Observer.* His not untypical response to their constant criticism was to buy the rival paper, the much older (founded 1855) *Harrow Gazette.*

But this paper was already on its last legs and readership was hardly helped by the new owner's insistence that they reprint his speeches virtually verbatim. By July 1921, the *Gazette* was losing so much money that Mosley was obliged to sell. The purchaser, unsurprisingly, was the *Harrow Observer* which henceforth became the *Harrow Observer & Gazette,* a title which it maintained on its masthead until comparatively recent times.

Mosley proved no more successful with his hard core Conservative supporters. In both the 1922 and 1923 elections he was obliged to stand as an Independent candidate and, although on both occasions he retained his seat, his majority was considerably reduced.

Ever mercurial, Mosley next switched allegiance to the Labour party only to find that his new sympathies were uncongenial to right-wing Harrow, prompting him to accept a nomination for Ladywood in Birmingham in 1924 (being beaten by just 77 votes by a certain Neville Chamberlain).

Mosley's subsequent career, during which he founded the notorious British Union of Fascists, took him far from Harrow and he was an old man before he was to return (privately) for meetings in the 1960s.

Dating from 1923, the old Harrow Baths at Charles Crescent was one of the prettiest pools for miles around.

Familiar South Harrow roads were just taking shape when these Roxeth Cubs were snapped c.1920. The background houses are in Kingsley Road with Wargrave Road and Scarsdale Road to the left and right.

Another very different personality also made headline news in the inter-war years.

This was the long-distance record flyer Amy Johnson who did much of her early flying from Stag Lane Aerodrome on the Harrow/Edgware border, also home to the newly founded de Havilland Aircraft Company.

It was at Stag Lane that Captain de Havilland built Britain's first truly successful aeroplane, the De Havilland Moth, which by 1926 was produced at the rate of virtually one a day.

Dubbed "the car of the air", it was flown by many celebrities, including the stage and film comedian Will Hay who kept his plane at Stag Lane.

In later years, Amy Johnson moved her home to Stanmore while working for the Air Transport Auxiliary, a job which tragically ended in an accident over the Thames Estuary in 1941.

Today, a commemorative plaque recalls her temporary home at Vernon Court. The so-called Aerodrome Estate also boasts a Mollison Way, named after Jim Mollison, the fellow pilot she married in 1932, as well as a de Havilland Road.

As befitted a growing town, Harrow now underwent a change in local government status. By amalgamating the old urban districts of Harrow on the Hill and Wealdstone with the parishes of Pinner, Harrow Weald and Great and Little Stanmore, it became the more powerful Harrow Urban District Council. Coincidentally, as those with a taste for history were quick to comment, its new boundaries – Wembley and Stanmore apart – were virtually identical to those of the old Domesday Manor of Harrow.

In a book of modest scale, it would be impossible to attempt to list all the many buildings and institutions established or enlarged during the between-wars years but mention should, at least, be made of one that eventually provoked many years of controversy.

Since 1855, there had been a highly successful gas works in Roxeth, just off Northolt Road. Although it had inevitably grown over the years, it was generally viewed in a favourable light – even the sometimes offensive smells were tolerated and children with whooping cough were actually encouraged to play around the purifier, as its fumes were considered beneficial.

Then, at the end of the 1920s, against considerable local opposition, the gas company of the day decided to erect a gas holder that was 240ft high, with a diameter of 162ft and a capacity of 4 million cubic feet. Visible for miles and seriously spoiling the traditional view towards Windsor from the hilltop St. Mary's, the gasometer was everyone's pet hate.

Some attempt was made to camouflage it during World War II but, in post-war years, a large "NO" painted on its side drew even more attention to its bulk. Whether this was intended as a simple negative – or shorthand for Northolt Airport – the sign's presence had been rendered necessary by an extraordinary incident in which the pilot of a large commercial plane, ignoring conventional navigational aids, confused the Roxeth gas holder with the one at Southall. He therefore put his plane down at Northolt Airport rather than his proper close-to-Southall destination at Heathrow.

To conclude the story, Roxeth finally lost its holder in 1986. There were few to bemoan its loss and, by the 1990s, the whole of the gas-works site had been swallowed up by office buildings and a Waitrose supermarket.

On a more positive note, the between-wars years gave Stanmore the nationally known Royal National Orthopaedic Hospital on the site of an earlier convalescent home for sick children and the present Queen Mother (as Duchess of York) accompanied the Duke to open the Stuart Memorial extension to Harrow Hospital on Roxeth Hill. (They returned, too, a few years later, to open the new terraced gardens in front of Druries on Harrow Hill.)

More controversially, Stanmore Park, one of the area's greatest houses, was acquired by the Royal Air Force in 1938 and pulled down to make way for Barrage Balloon Command.

And, of course, there were new cinemas everywhere, for this was the golden age of movie-going. They included the Harrow Coliseum in Station Road, opened in 1920 by Lady Mosley; the Dominion (now the Safari), opened in January 1936; and the Granada in Sheepcote Road, opened in October 1937, by movie star Jessie Matthews, who later became a Hatch End resident.

Harrow could even lay claim to one of the great Hollywood stars of the day, George Arliss, whose parents lived at the long-since-demolished Wealdstone Cottage near the site of the present Harrow Weald bus garage. Arliss, who won the first-ever Best Actor Academy Award in 1929, died in 1946. Despite having made his career largely in America, the Arliss family evidently felt he should be buried as close as possible to his parents who lie in the so-called New Cemetery opposite All Saints, Harrow Weald. Possibly because of his fame, the funeral was kept very private and no account appeared in the local press nevertheless movie buffs can find his grave not in the New Cemetery but in a plot in the council cemetery just a stone's throw from the church.

An anonymity he rarely knew in life is now compounded by the tombstone's simple inscription which totally ignores George Arliss, actor, for the more modest George Arliss, M.A., Columbia University, New York, U.S.A.

Though he never actually lived in our midst, the three-times Wimbledon Singles champion Fred Perry was at one time a frequent visitor to Harrow where he belonged to the Herga Lawn Tennis Club. Having claimed the very first men's and women's Wimbledon champions, (Spencer Gore and Maud Watson) the previous century, the town also enjoyed a further link with the Championships when Jean Nicoll, who attended St. Margaret's School in Sheepcote Road, achieved a brief blaze of glory being the magazine *Picture Post*'s cover girl in its 1939 Wimbledon issue at the tender age of 16. Unhappily, the magazine's appraisal of her talent – "said to be as good as Lenglen at her age" – was never truly put to the test since the outbreak of war in September 1939 necessarily put a halt to the annual Wimbledon event: nevertheless, as Mrs Jean Bostock, she returned after the war, reaching the quarter finals in 1946, 1947 and 1948.

36. Harrow at War again

From the vantage point of the 1990s, it is almost impossible to believe that, less than 21 years after the Armistice that marked the end of the 1914–18 conflict, the world went to war again.

This time, too, it was a total war in which tens of thousands on the Home Front were required to make sacrifices every bit as awesome as those demanded of our servicemen and women.

Though the phrase "Don't you know there's a war on?" was frequently used (invariably as a put-down), it was, in truth, a genuinely rhetorical remark. Faced with stringent rationing (not just of food but of clothing, coal, petrol and other essentials), severe shortages, night time black-outs, not to mention the multiple requirements of home defence, Harrow's residents, whether young or old, could never forget that the days – and ways – of peace were far behind them.

Though, as you can read elsewhere, the air raid sirens that sounded within minutes of the declaration of war were happily proved to be a false alarm, the ever-present threat of attack from the air meant that thousands were soon involved in the grim realities of what began, simply, as Air Raid Precautions but which ultimately became the more comprehensive service of Civil Defence.

Later, the hardly less real possibility of invasion from the skies led to the formation of an armed force, known originally as the Local Defence Volunteers but now affectionately remembered as the Home Guard (or even Dad's Army). The day set by the government for enrolment happened to fall on the day of the annual Pinner Fair and older residents can still recall the long queue of applicants that formed outside Pinner Police Station virtually oblivious of the entertainments all around them.

Harrow's relative proximity to London, not to mention the existence of several likely targets (e.g. Fighter Command HQ, Kodak Ltd), within its own boundaries, prompted many families to evacuate their children to areas of presumed safety. Some 150 youngsters, for example, went to Kodak's American hometown of Rochester, New York.

Curiously enough, at the same time, many City companies moved out to Harrow.

Another unexpected arrival in our midst was Malvern College from the Herefordshire countryside.

As early as 1938, Malvern's Head Master had been told that, in the event of war, their premises would be required "as a matter of national interest". Only later was it known that Malvern had been selected to house the Admiralty if the latter's London base were to be devastated in the anticipated raids. Although this particular contingency never arose, in April 1942, Malvern College still had to move at virtually a moment's notice. Its new occupants were a top-secret radar research establishment which British Intelligence had every reason to

Barclays Bank in High Street, Wealdstone, was severely damaged in an August 1940 air raid.

believe was to be bombed into oblivion at the next full moon.

For a variety of reasons, Harrow School was to prove the perfect host for the Malvern homeless. Its pupil numbers were at a low ebb, since many parents not unnaturally wanted their boys at home in times of danger and several of the boarding houses had already been requisitioned for war-time purposes. Among them were Newlands in Harrow Park, which became a temporary hospital, and West Acre, in London Road, which for a time was used by the Coldstream Guards.

It was in these unusual circumstances that Malvern boys moved in with their Harrow counterparts, earning the plaudits of Old Harrovian Prime Minister Winston Churchill, who, on a November 1942 visit, heartened both schools by likening them to "two famous regiments that serve side by side in a famous brigade".

Other local schools suffered similar inconvenience. Harrow Girls' County School, the forerunner of today's Greenhill College, was initially taken over by the government and only a personal appeal to the House of Commons by its redoubtable Head Mistress, Mary Huskisson, ensured its eventual reopening.

As it happened, the war dragged on for nearly 12 months before the first bombs dropped in Harrow.

Although early suggestions to tunnel out parts of the Hill as air raid shelters had proved impractical, most people now had access to reasonably adequate shelters – in the streets, in the parks and in the home, where most people's choice lay between the two government-sponsored alternatives, the indoor Morrison or the garden-built Anderson.

A few local residents succumbed to opportunistic advertisers promoting custom-built shelters with messages urging them to order now "before it's too late!"

Wealdstone was, in fact, the first area to be struck when, on an August night in 1940, a stick of 12 bombs fell in and around the High Street. Although Barclays Bank at the junction with Locket Road was virtually destroyed and buildings on either side extensively damaged, there were happily no fatalities on this occasion.

Two months later, however, eight people were killed and a further eight injured when bombs fell on Long Elmes and Edward Road, Harrow Weald.

The anxiety created by such raids was, if anything, aggravated by the security black-out which allowed the press to print only the most generalised of reports.

Even if describing a raid on its own doorstep, the *Harrow Observer* was still obliged to refer to "an incident on the outskirts of London".

Only if you knew a district intimately might you recognise it from the clues provided: for example, reported damage to "a cinema, a police court and an elementary school" in October 1940 clearly suggested the Wealdstone end of Station Road. Here bombs not only caused considerable damage but killed four Air Force personnel, who were waiting for a bus, and two girls sheltering in a telephone kiosk.

Occasionally, fuller details were released long after the incident concerned. A case in

Brick street shelter in Pinner High Street.

Underground shelter entrance in Roxeth Recreation Ground.
A snapshot donated by Mrs D. M. Edwards.

point was the belated announcement that a shower of incendiary bombs had hit the roof of the parish church of St. Mary's, without penetrating or damaging its famous 15th-century timbers.

Raids or no, some approximation of normal life had to be maintained and, after a temporary closure, the many local cinemas – then the nation's primary source of entertainment – were reopened. Each of the major cinema chains seems to have had its own way of dealing with air raid warnings.

Managers of the Granada circuit, which had opened a cinema in Sheepcote Road only eleven months before the war began, were provided with a code word which would alert them to the approach of enemy aircraft. It was then the manager's personal decision whether to continue the programme or to evacuate the building with the attendant risk of putting hundreds of people on the streets.

In any event, once the sirens had sounded, a public warning was always flashed on to the screen so that patrons could leave for their homes, if they wished.

Happily, no Harrow cinema ever received a direct hit although there was a near miss from a parachute mine which drifted dangerously over the two Station Road cinemas before being caught in the Kodak defensive system where, fortunately, it failed to explode.

Human nature being what it is, patrons who left the cinema of their own volition were not above asking for free entry on their next visit: after all, they argued, they had been unable to see the entire programme which, in those pre-television days, invariably consisted of a double bill of feature films, a newsreel and possibly a cartoon or short.

Just when most people were cheerfully subscribing to the motto "Britain Can Take It", there came a fresh horror to test their endurance.

Officially known as the V1 or, more colloquially, as "the doodlebug", this was literally a flying bomb that "doodled" its way over our towns, making a characteristic noise in flight, not dissimilar to a motor cycle engine. Its menace was intensified by the fact that no-one ever knew when the engine would cut out and the bomb would fall. One thing was certain. If the noise stopped, an explosion would quickly follow – and somewhere in your immediate vicinity.

One that landed in Kenton Lane in July 1944, caused one of the war's saddest casualties – a baby only seven hours old.

Because of its limited range, the flying bomb was only a threat to the south of England and many Harrow residents found this an opportune time to move – albeit temporarily – to friends elsewhere in the country; indeed, the *Harrow Observer* claimed in August 1944, that some 22,000 people had left the district in the previous few months.

They thus escaped an even greater menace. In September 1944, the Germans launched a new weapon – the so-called V2 – not a bomb, but a rocket missile which gave its victims no warning at all. It simply exploded, usually causing substantial casualties and damage, as at Uppingham Avenue, Belmont, in March 1945, when nine people died and 30 were injured.

The Operations Room at Bentley Priory from which Britain's air defences were directed.

Only fifteen V1 bombs actually landed in Harrow, although older residents will never forget hearing – and fearing – the many more that passed overhead on their trail of destruction.

While a full history of Harrow's air raids remains to be written, the Pinner Association has provided ample compensation in its publication *Pinner At War* which, among other fascinating details, records that over 1200 air raid alerts were sounded in the Pinner area. Given that the average duration of each alert was one and a quarter hours, this means that the good folk of Pinner spent no fewer than a full two months – days and nights – under threat from the air: an amazing figure which would almost certainly have been mirrored throughout the whole of Harrow.

Once it was no longer a matter of national security, Harrow's Surveyors' Department were able to release a chart of enemy activity which showed that, between August 1940 and March 1945, the district had been the victim of 509 German bombs and four parachute mines, one of which, as we have read, failed to explode. Twenty-five of the bombs also failed to go off.

That the raids were not infinitely worse – and that Britain was never subjugated by German air attack and eventual invasion – was, to a very large extent, due to the air defence conducted right in our midst at Fighter Command Headquarters at Stanmore.

Founded with what now seems remarkable prescience, Fighter Command under Air Vice Marshal Sir Hugh Dowding took over the famous old mansion of Bentley Priory (see Chapter 27), as early as July 1936, some three years before No. 3 Balloon Centre was formed at Stanmore Park.

Dowding, a widower who lived with his sister in a now vanished Stanmore house called Montrose, quickly realised that, as it stood, the grand mansion was hardly equal to the challenge of its new role.

So, long before war broke out, the two largest rooms had become the Operations Room and the Filter Room, the conservatory had given way to a veritable warren of wooden outbuildings and, most important of all, work had started on an underground Operations Block.

According to RAF records, some 58,270 tons of earth were dug out and some 225,000 tons of concrete poured in. Soon, the original white stucco mansion was covered in green and brown camouflage paint although there appears to have been grave doubts about its effectiveness. At one time, there were even plans to make the building look derelict and so persuade the enemy that Fighter Command had moved elsewhere.

Although this plan was never carried out, it remains a curious fact that no concentrated enemy attack was ever made against the Priory. The only recorded damage was done, in succession, by two small bombs, which fell near the married quarters, and by blasts from both a flying bomb and a V2 rocket.

Tragically, the only real threat to the building was made by one of our own aircraft. A Wellington of No. 311 (Czech) Squadron seems to have lost its way returning from a raid on Bremen and, with fuel dangerously low, attempted to crash land in the Priory's gardens. Most of the crew were able to bale out in time but of the two men who gallantly stayed aboard,

"HMS Pinner" on a fund-raising trip down Pinner High Street during Warship Week, March, 1943.

VE Day Party in Wargrave Road, South Harrow. Photograph donated by Mrs Edwards.

the navigator was killed and the pilot badly burned on impact.

As the authority responsible for air raid warnings, it fell to Bentley Priory to create the first great shock of the war when it caused the air raid sirens to be sounded within minutes of the Prime Minister's radio announcement that war had begun. There were, in fact, no enemy aircraft overhead but, in those early days, the siren was sounded on the approach of any aircraft not positively identified as friendly.

Even less well-known is the fact that Bletchley Park, the Buckinghamshire mansion famed for its code-breaking work, maintained two "bombe" stations in our locality, one in London Road, Stanmore, the other in Eastcote Road, Eastcote. At a time when only one of the very first computers could fill an entire room, the "bombes" – used to simulate the operations carried out in the German "Enigma" machine – were up to 18ft tall, 12ft wide and at least 3ft deep. They were also extremely noisy and, before producing any usable material, would tick loudly; hence the term "bombe".

Given the top secret nature of the work, both local stations were heavily guarded and a complete security black-out imposed on members of the Women's Royal Naval Service who ran the machines. Their silence later won the compliment of Winston Churchill who, with characteristic humour, thanked "the chickens for laying so well without clucking".

By the time the war had entered its final years, "make do" had become a way of life.

Marriage ceremonies, for example, had to make do without iced cakes, their manufacture and sale being banned under the Sugar (Restrictions and Use) Order. Nor could confetti be thrown, since paper was on the ration - or, for that matter, rice since all foodstuffs were in far too short a supply to waste.

So many other delicacies disappeared "under the counter" for the pleasure of a chosen few that a writer in the *Hatch End Bulletin* felt compelled to sing the praises of the manageress of the Cut & Quality Store in Uxbridge Road. Beaming at her customers, this splendid lady would apparently assure them that there was "nothing under the counter, except my feet".

Inevitably, there were times when frustration boiled over into anger, as when a thoughtless War Department allocated a number of empty houses in the district for use by Italian prisoners-of-war.

Believing that such homes should more properly be given to London's bombed-out homeless, local residents organised such a vehement protest (even taken up by the national press), that the War Department was obliged to retract their decision.

Many prisoners-of-war nevertheless spent long years of captivity in Harrow. The largest number were held at Rayners Lane where land intended for council housing, and already provided with roads and basic services, was hastily transformed into a P.O.W. camp. At its peak, this camp housed upward of 1100 Germans, including many Afrika Corps and SS men, of whom some 50 per cent were assessed as being "ardent Nazis".

A further camp for some 500, largely Italian, prisoners was run on an 11-acre site

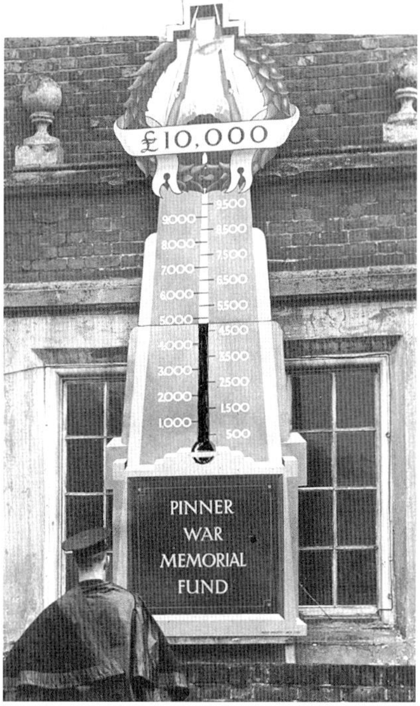

Pinner's War Memorial Fund target on the one-time Marsh Road school-house.

The VE Day party for children of the Pinnerwood Park Estate in May, 1945.

between Oxhey Lane and Uxbridge Road, Harrow Weald, the site of today's Roger Bannister Sports Centre. Non-fraternisation was, of course, the order of the day but it was not always fully obeyed.

Peter Carroll, who spent the war years in nearby Hampden Road, was one who later recalled in the local press how he and his friends had regularly shared tea with prisoners "through the barbed wire". Since tea was still very much on the ration, one can only assume that it was the prisoners' tea that they shared!

With rationing continuing well into the first years of peace, many families turned with relief to the government-sponsored British Restaurants set up in improvised premises to provide simple but nutritious meals.

Between 1941 and 1944, no fewer than nine were opened locally – in Wealdstone, Queensbury, South Harrow, Central Harrow, Stanmore, Pinner, Rayners Lane, North Harrow and Belmont Circle. Possibly the most popular was the Central Harrow restaurant, conveniently located in an earlier Victoria Hall, adjoining St. John's, Greenhill, in Station Road.

To contemporary eyes, the restaurants' most striking feature was their cheapness. When the Pinner branch opened in Bennetts Park in 1943, a main meal (comprising meat or fish and two vegetables) was offered at six old pence, roughly equivalent to 2½p of current currency. In a surprising precursor of today's ubiquitous take-away, it was even possible to take your meals back home.

When Victory in Europe finally came in May 1945, Harrow's celebrations ranged from traditional thanksgiving services to the hanging of a Hitler effigy from a gibbet in Sussex Road. But, behind it all lay the knowledge that there was still the war against Japan to be won.

Indeed, it was not until August of that year that our world began to return if not to normality (for there were long years of austerity ahead), at least to peace.

Those who had been away from Harrow probably found the town relatively little changed in its appearance. The major transformations were still to come. But, in almost every other way, they returned to a very different world from the one they had left.

Confirmation of this change quickly came in the summer of 1945 when, within two months of the resignation of the wartime coalition government, Labour won a landslide General Election.

By one of those intriguing coincidences that so much delight writers of local history, the Old Harrovian Winston Churchill was now succeeded by one who could conveniently be called a Newer Harrovian. For Clement Attlee, the man who so soundly trounced him at the polls, had been quietly living in our midst since 1931 in a house called Heywood in London Road, Stanmore.

Sir Winston Churchill, seen with Lady Churchill and Head Master A. P. Boissier, so enjoyed his visit to Harrow in 1940 that he returned year after year.

37. Harrow's first Freeman

During the years of World War II and possibly the two decades that followed, anyone wishing to identify Harrow to an outsider had only to say "where Winston Churchill went to school", for the place to receive immediate recognition and, usually, instant approval.

So, once Harrow had become a borough – as distinct from a mere Urban District – in 1954, it seemed only appropriate that it should choose Sir Winston as its first Freeman.

Thus, on a memorable day in September 1955, the great and the good of the district attended a banquet in the now-vanished Kodak Hall and saw the grand old man receive the town's freedom together with a handsome inscribed goblet made by Wealdstone's Whitefriars Glass works.

Although, as we shall see, it was by no means his last appearance in Harrow, the event marked one further stage in the former premier's on-and-off relationship with Harrow School and Harrow Town which began with his entry to the School in April 1888.

As the Churchill historian, Jim Golland, reminds us in one of his many fascinating publications, Churchill was originally destined for Eton, like other members of the celebrated Marlborough family; however, a bout of pneumonia, whilst at preparatory school, had convinced his parents that he should avoid the dampness of the Thames at Eton and enjoy instead the fresh air of high and healthy Harrow.

Golland also convincingly gives the lie to the oft-repeated claim that Churchill was a near-duffer at school: certainly, he was an unusual and sometimes unpredictable pupil who, among other escapades, is said to have exploded a home-made bomb in the well of the deserted (and reputedly haunted) Roxeth House off then West Street cricket fields. Supposedly, he was also the only boy to volunteer when a celebrated swordsman sought to demonstrate his skill by slicing through an apple placed on a pupil's head!

The schoolboy Churchill was a regular contributor to the school magazine, the *Harrovian*, recording, among many diverse subjects, his pleasure at the lectures given to the school by some of the most interesting personalities of the 1880s, including the actors Henry Irving and Ellen Terry and the American explorer, H.M. Stanley.

For all his confidence and drive, he could hardly have foreseen that, within eight years of his leaving the Head Master's House in December 1892, he would, himself, be lecturing in Speech Room on his experiences in the Boer War.

As shown in the film *Young Winston* (for which many scenes were actually shot at Harrow), Churchill had been sent to South Africa as a war correspondent for the *Morning Post*, had been captured, and then escaped in especially stirring circumstances.

During his subsequent rise to political fame, Churchill's relationship with his old school seems to have cooled, possibly because his association with some unpopular government

Harry Woodbridge and his West Street staff are said to have rescued young Winston from the effects of a home-made bomb.

Churchill's first Harrow boarding house was the now largely demolished Garlands in Peterborough Road.

measures once caused him to be booed by Harrow boys. Nevertheless, by 1938, he was sufficiently reconciled to come to Harrow to judge the annual reading prize.

It was during World War II, however, that he first began to find real joy – and, as he himself often remarked, real inspiration – from his visits to the school.

Shortly after the start of Christmas term, 1940, some 300 incendiary bombs were dropped – or, more precisely, were jettisoned – over the school, falling in a line across the playing fields, the parade ground, the Museum Schools, Speech Room and The Grove. Both the Museum Schools and Speech Room caught alight although the fires were quickly controlled, first by the school's own fire service, and then by the local brigade (although Speech Room and its organ suffered considerable damage).

When news of the bombing reached Churchill (possibly through his Private Secretary, John Colville, another Old Harrovian), he promptly sent a telegram of sympathy to Head Master Paul Boissier.

Emboldened by this gesture of friendship, Boissier immediately pondered the chances of getting the great man (who had become Prime Minister earlier that year) to pay a personal visit to the school.

After considerable negotiation, Churchill agreed to hear a performance of the School Songs, providing he could choose his particular favourites. Because of wartime national security, Boissier was able to inform only two of his staff of the impending visit, the music master and a certain Mr Plumtree who, virtually overnight, was asked to write an additional verse in praise of Churchill for the song "Stet Fortuna Domus" (the school's motto which, very roughly, translates as "Let the fortune of our house endure").

It is an interesting comment on the dominance of Harrow on the political scene of the day that, when Churchill duly arrived (in December 1940), he was accompanied not only by his Old Harrovian brother Jack, but also by four senior members of his administration – Old Harrovians to a man. Had the Attorney General of the day been available, the number would have been even higher, contrasting greatly with the late 1990s when, to the best of the writer's knowledge, there is not a single Old Harrovian in the House of Commons.

The Songs proved a triumph for all concerned. Seated on the stage of Speech Room in front of a curtain that masked the recent bomb damage, Churchill was visibly moved by the singing and warmly approved (with one amendment) the new verse which initially read as follows:

"Nor less we praise in darker days
The leader of our nation
And Churchill's name shall win acclaim
From each new generation.
For you have power in danger's hour
Our freedom to defend, Sir,
Though long the fight, we know the right
Will triumph in the end, Sir."

The schoolboy Winston photographed on the gates of Roxeth House.

Churchill continued to visit Harrow until a few years before his death in 1965.

Given his well-known optimism, Churchill's amendment was not untypical – he simply asked for the word "sterner" to be substituted for "darker" in the opening line.

From this one visit, a long tradition was born, Churchill returning to hear School Songs virtually every year until 1961 when he was well into his late eighties.

He died in 1965 at the age of 90 and the songs he loved so much were subsequently rechristened Churchill Songs in his honour. Similarly, the craft, design and technology centre built on Grove Hill in the late 1980s is now called Churchill Schools.

Against this background, it is surprising, to say the least, that his first school home – Garlands in Peterborough Road – has never been commemorated and now survives only as a façade to a modern apartment block.

To those in the know, however, some slight amends have recently been made. The previously unnamed slip road opposite the house is now known as Davidson Lane in belated recognition of H.O. Davidson, the very first house-master of Harrow's very first Freeman.

As Harrow's first Freeman, Churchill was given this locally-made goblet.

In this Odhams News photo, Rev. John Richards, then vicar of St. John's, Greenhill, stands alone amid the three-train wreckage of the Wealdstone Train Disaster.

38. Disaster and Triumph

Though the 1951 Festival of Britain did its considerable best to convince us otherwise, the early 1950s were essentially years of austerity for us all, with many goods still on ration and men of fighting age required to complete an even longer period of National Service (due to the war in Korea).

Making the days even grimmer, the middle of 1952 witnessed a sequence of tragic disasters. First, in August, a flash flood in Lynmouth, Devon, killed 36 people, to be followed the very next month by a jet crash at the Farnborough Air Show which resulted in 28 fatalities.

Yet terrible as they were, both of these events were dwarfed by the horrors of Wednesday, October 8th, 1952, to be forever remembered as the day of the Wealdstone Train Disaster in which a staggering 112 people perished.

For all that millions of words have been written about it, younger generations may well need to know the basic outlines of the catastrophe which happened at 7.31 on a slightly foggy morning.

A local commuter train travelling from Tring to Euston had just drawn into Platform 4 when it was struck by an express train from Perth with such force that the three rear coa ches of the local train were smashed to splinters. Inevitably the impact derailed the express which, moments later, was itself struck by another express en route for the North.

The ensuing wreckage, which rose some 30ft high, partially demolishing the overhead passenger bridge, will never be forgotten by those who saw it, including the writer who was a top-deck passenger on a bus that passed the station within hours of the disaster.

Despite a superhuman rescue and salvage effort that involved not only the expected services but the Salvation Army, the Women's Voluntary Service and the USAF from Ruislip, it was almost 48 hours before the last victim was taken from the wreckage and over four days and three nights before the line could be cleared.

Given that the driver and fireman of the Perth express were both killed, the subsequent enquiry was unable to state precisely why they had seemingly ignored signals at danger. In any event, from a distance of almost 50 years, it now looks as if the scale of the disaster was largely the outcome of several cruel and unpredictable twists of fate.

The local train, for example, was two coaches longer than usual – and, moreover, densely packed – because of the cancellation of another train.

Largely due to foggy conditions earlier that morning, the Perth–Euston express was over 80 minutes behind schedule at the time of the accident. The Euston–Liverpool train was also running about five minutes late, a combination of circumstances that, tragically, brought all three trains to the same spot at virtually the same time.

Perhaps surprisingly, the disaster was actually the third accident on the same line to pro-

Many died on the overhead passenger bridge (seen here c.1911) when it was broken in two by a pile-up of wrecked coaches.

Aerial view of the disaster scene.

The late Duke of Gloucester (left) presents a Charter to the former Urban District of Harrow, elevating it to the status of a Borough.

Civic dignitaries pose on the steps of Harrow School's Old Schools after the first Civic Service of the new Borough.

Four-minute miler Roger Bannister as a small boy, seen with big sister Joyce in their Harrow garden. The family lived first in Butler Road, later moving to Whitmore Road.

Sir Roger Bannister returns to Harrow in September 1966, to open the Bannister Sports Centre in Uxbridge Road.

duce fatalities, the first being as early as November 1840 when, in a curious anticipation of events to come, a derailed train was hit by another.

Thirty years later, seven people were killed when a broken coupling mistakenly left part of a coal train on the down line where it, too, was struck by a Euston–Liverpool express.

Significantly, all three accidents happened in October–November in an era when polluted air frequently brought fogs and smogs, such as the great "pea-souper" which, in December 1952, was supposed to have claimed, directly or indirectly, the lives of some 4000 Londoners.

Two years after the train disaster, Harrow was again back in the headlines – this time, however, in an infinitely happier context.

At Iffley Road, Oxford, on a May day in 1954, Roger Bannister, a one-time pupil of Vaughan Road Infants and Junior Schools, was the first man to smash the mythical barrier of a four-minute mile.

Though his record was, in truth, eclipsed within 45 days, it remained a tremendous achievement at a time when food rationing had only just ended and sports facilities, especially for runners, were virtually non-existent. Bannister himself was later to admit that much of his practice running had been done at night over private land on which technically he was a trespasser.

To ensure that his successors enjoyed an easier route to athletic success, he devoted part of the royalties of a best-selling book about his achievement to the provision of a proper training ground and, in September 1966, he had the satisfaction of opening the present Bannister Sports Centre in Uxbridge Road.

The sixties saw the birth of boutiques like "The in Scene" in Station Road.

39. The Swinging Sixties

Even those with very clear memories of the decade would probably find it hard to say if Harrow truly swung in the Swinging Sixties. Undeniably, it moved about a bit, unleashing a wave of change that subsequently engulfed what we once knew as Greenhill but are now encouraged to call Central Harrow.

In fact, anyone leaving the town in the mid 1960s and returning for the first time today might feel totally lost, since so many familiar landmarks have long since disappeared.

This process of change, though it picked up speed throughout the sixties, had probably begun as early as 1955 with the death of Sir Alfred Denville, proprietor of the Harrow Coliseum, the very handsome theatre in Station Road. In his will, Sir Alfred stipulated that the building be sold as quickly as possible.

Though stage performances continued for a while – the last being the noted comedian (and local resident) Leslie Henson, in a play called *Small Hotel*, in June 1956 – no theatrical entrepreneur could be found with the money to match the sums offered by the now-burgeoning supermarket chains. Despite a public inquiry, in which the Harrow Arts Council put a convincing case for the theatre's retention, the site went – for what now seems a miserly £67,500 – to Premier Supermarkets.

So the town lost a priceless facility, along with a building which, with its twin minarets, had been an attractive feature of the local street scene for nearly four decades.

Having been elevated from a mere urban district to a borough in 1954, Harrow attained London Borough status in April 1965. With this added impetus, progress was now accelerated on a Central Harrow Development Plan from which the town was intended to emerge as an office and shopping centre of the first rank.

The first obvious result was the transformation of the quiet residential streets behind Station Road – notably Lyon Road and St. John's Road – into a virtually continuous office block whose multi-storeys, rising high above the Station Road shops, were to change forever Harrow's familiar skyline.

Simultaneously, the Local Authority set about acquiring a proper home for itself and its staff, a project which (the war years apart) had been under more or less continuous discussion since 1934 when the council of that time decided that its offices, scattered throughout the district, should be brought together under one roof.

Of a limited choice of sites, the area adjoining Harrow and Wealdstone station traditionally known as Poets' Corner (from the number of its roads named after famous writers) proved to be the most favoured.

As it proved, the choice of site was relatively easy compared to the difficulties of choosing a design and, in 1962, the scheme received a severe set-back when the neo-Georgian

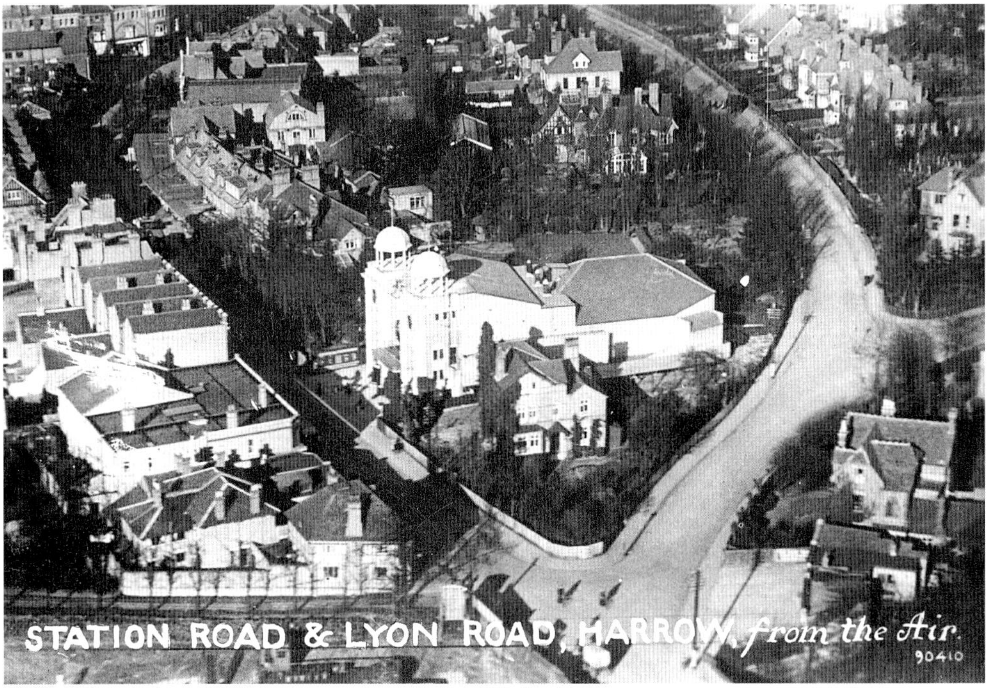

Aerial view of the Harrow that began to vanish in the sixties, showing the Harrow Coliseum surrounded by elegant homes.

In 1967, the Essoldo at Belmont Circle joined the legion of lost cinemas that included every local Odeon.

Known as Poet's Corner, an entire area of Wealdstone including the Bridge Schools was cleared for the Civic Centre.

The prize-winning design for the Civic Centre originally featured a theatre and halls block (right).

Part of "green" Harrow disappears as Northwick Park Golf Club and its surrounding land is ploughed under for the new hospital's foundation.

Local residents get an unexpected close-up of the Queen following the 1970 opening of Northwick Park Hospital.

plans of the chosen architect were rejected both by the council and by public opinion as being far too traditional. This was, after all, the sixties!

When somebody suggested a design competition, the idea was enthusiastically received and, in truth, Harrow could hardly have chosen a more distinguished trio of judges than Sir Basil Spence, newly famous for rebuilding Coventry Cathedral, Sir Hugh Casson and Professor A. Douglas Jones.

Nevertheless it was 1969 before a tender was accepted and 1972 before any of the council's employees were able to move in.

Today, opinion inevitably differs as to the attractiveness if not the effectiveness of this so-called Civic Centre. Although the "bold profiles of pre-cast concrete" now look very much of their period, in general the building does not disappoint Basil Spence's expressed desire that it would be "a pleasure to see, not just a place in which one pays rent".

The original scheme, however, envisaged a second wing incorporating both a large assembly hall and a small experimental theatre. Some 30 years later, this still remains unbuilt in a town that now, more than ever, desperately needs a proper theatre for the public at large.

The late sixties also saw work commence on a new hospital for the district.

Although greatly extended during the 1930s, Harrow Hospital on Roxeth Hill had been opened as early in the century as 1906 and was becoming sorely out-moded and over-stretched.

This time, however, ample room was allowed for the inevitable expansion since the chosen site – off the Watford Road and swallowing up the Northwick Park Golf Club – occupied well over 46 acres.

Here, after some four years of continuous work, arose the nucleus of the present Northwick Park Hospital, received with considerable acclaim in British and European architectural circles for its venturesome lay-out in which the standard concept of a single building was replaced by a series of buildings connected by its own internal "street system".

Further indication of the building's importance was provided by its 1970 opening which was performed by the Queen herself before a distinguished audience including the then relatively little known Margaret Thatcher.

Though other interesting buildings rose in our midst in the sixties, not least the light and airy public library in Gayton Road, the decade is equally remembered for the buildings that were lost, among them the Odeon cinemas at Kenton and Wealdstone, the Embassy at North Harrow and the Essoldo at Belmont Circle.

As audiences continued to desert "the pictures" for the home-based attractions of "the box", other cinema casualties followed in the early 1970s, including the South Harrow and Kingsbury Odeons and the Rex, Northwood Hills.

A notable survivor – to this very day – is the one-time Odeon at Rayners Lane. Although it no longer functions as a cinema, it continues as a so-called "cine-bar" and, having been officially listed for its splendid 1930s architectural detail, it is now spared the threat of demolition.

Believe it or not, it's former Pinner County School pupil Elton John (born Reg Dwight), photographed at the family home in Northwood Hills in 1969.

40. The Transformation Continues

For all the connotations of frivolity inherent in the term "swinging sixties", the decade, in fact, launched a number of serious initiatives which have since become a (perhaps grudgingly accepted) part of our daily lives.

In no particular sequence, Harrow in the sixties saw its first genuine supermarket (Sainsbury's in South Harrow), its first self-service petrol pumps (at a North Harrow garage) and, following the lead given nationally, the first parking meters, traffic wardens and breathalyser tests, not forgetting the division of our postal district into post code numbers which, to this day, many still have difficulty in remembering.

The first Hoppa-style single-decker buses also began to appear in our streets although this was little consolation to those who had regularly used the single-track Harrow-Stanmore railway line, opened in 1890 and finally closed to all traffic, both passenger and goods, in 1964.

There was particular sorrow, too, at the loss of the picturesque Stanmore station which, except for the frontage to Gordon Avenue was finally demolished in July 1970.

Meanwhile, on the popular music scene, it can be said that the borough virtually gave birth to two very familiar names. In 1964, impresario Kit Lambert discovered the group that was to become The Who performing – apparently on a stage of beer crates – at the Railway Tavern adjoining the Wealdstone railway bridge. Simultaneously, a former Pinner County School pupil, then living in Northwood Hills, was beginning a truly phenomenal career that was to transform him from the humble Reg Dwight of his birth to today's iconic Sir Elton John.

The local entertainment scene was also greatly enlivened in 1961 with the launch of the annual Harrow Show whose very British mixture of all-family pursuits continues to delight thousands every August Bank Holiday weekend, wet or dry.

For the rest, the sixties and seventies were perhaps most notable for the continued transformation of what were, traditionally, Harrow's two main shopping streets, College Road and Station Road.

The first – and most modest – of what proved to be a whole sequence of bus stations in College Road arose in 1971 opposite the still-standing Heathfield School and Grange Furnishing Stores (later seriously damaged by fire). But, by the end of the seventies, both had made way for the town's first shopping mall, the £21 million (or so the papers said) St. Ann's Centre, officially opened by Diana, Princess of Wales, in November 1987.

Around the same time, St. Ann's Road (which held another entrance to the mall) was largely pedestrianised.

Both projects were officially considered to be "illustrations of Harrow's move to combat any drift of shoppers to other rival areas".

The undoubted success of the St. Ann's Centre, however, inevitably meant a drift of shop-

A very different College Road as it looked in September 1969, the day Harrow became a pay-as-you-park town. Note the lock-up shops and garden centre on the left and Grange Furnishing Stores on the right.

Landmarks in Central Harrow of the early 1960s, the colonnaded bank (centre) and the old Baptist church (right) have long since disappeared.

A town in transition – the recently built office block in Lyon Road towers above the soon-to-be-demolished Harrow Technical College.

Once a popular shopping street,
Clarendon Road is now a concrete "canyon" between an office block and a multi-storey car park.

The Afro meets the short-back-and-sides as the Schools' Action Union, advocates of "Pupil Power", seek to recruit boys from Harrow School.

The face of British football over 30 years ago – England's World Cup Squad of the late 1960s during a training session at Vale Farm, Sudbury, football ground.

pers away from other shopping areas within Harrow itself with the consequent loss of many well-known retailers whose premises were taken by essentially short-term "sell it cheap" operations.

Older residents would also argue that the undoubted gain represented by the St. Ann's Centre was somewhat offset by the loss of the attractive Clarendon Road whose name alone survives.

Major changes to College Road continued well into the 1980s; first, with the redevelopment of the Baptist church whose familiar old building, complete with landmark tower, was re-built as part of an office block in 1982, and the creation of the (literally) gleaming First National House, adjoining the station, in 1989.

By comparison, the Central Harrow stretch of Station Road is still largely recognisable though what were once its most familiar buildings – the Harrow Coliseum and the Harrow Technical College and School of Art – have long since disappeared.

The decade also witnessed a total transformation of the old Sopers department store in which an impressive extension swallowed up adjoining properties, including the age-old Greenhill pub, the Marquis of Granby.

It was not, however, until 1972 that its name was finally changed to Debenhams, although the latter company had been associated with the store for many decades.

A few hundred yards away at the junction with the pedestrianised St. Ann's Road, the town later gained one of its most welcome "newcomers", an appealing bronze statue of a skipping girl named "Katie" after the daughter (and model) of the sculptor James Butler.

In another milestone of civic history,""Katie" was jointly unveiled by the Mayor of Harrow and his opposite number from the northern French town of Douai, with whom, in a gesture of European unity, our town was twinned in 1979.

By an amazing coincidence, as earlier chapters reveal, Douai was also the site of the 16th-century Catholic mission from which priests were daringly sent in disguise to Protestant England. It was, too, the town in which World War I hero, Leefe Robinson, was finally captured by the Germans.

The 1970s and 1980s also witnessed substantial changes in other parts of the borough such as the rise of the vast – and soon-to-be-vacated – A.A. headquarters in Stanmore Broadway and the loss of Pinner's historic schoolhouse and one-time library at the foot of Bridge Street.

Even Harrow Hill, despite the good efforts of the conservation society, the Harrow Hill Trust, was not without its seismic tremors.

The green slopes of Sudbury Hill proved especially vulnerable. While there was relatively little opposition to a private hospital (the aptly named Clementine Churchill) built by American Medical (Europe) Ltd at the Hill's base, there was considerable anger at the demolition of the old Calvary House Nursing Home at the top and its replacement by a vast apartment complex called – for some unfathomable reason – Chasewood Park. Ironically,

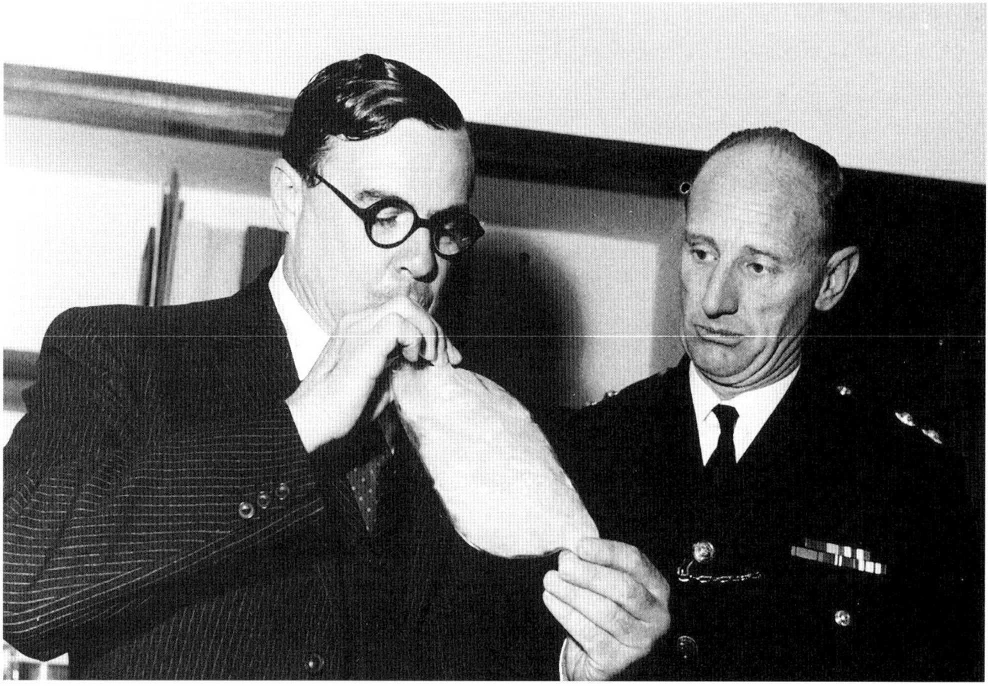

On the day the breathalyser was introduced in October 1967, John Page, MP for Harrow West, sportingly takes an experimental test. As the police chief obviously realises, the Member was "right on the margin".

Two years later, Lord Sainsbury personally checks out the customers at the company's first local self-service supermarket in Northolt Road, South Harrow.

the chapel of this one-time convent has survived, having been earlier listed as a work of Giles Gilbert Scott, grandson of the earlier Scott who left so many fine buildings on the Hill.

In the circumstances, one can only wonder what these eminent architects would have thought of its deconsecration for use as a leisure centre for the occupants of the neighbouring flats.

Nor did residents ever expect to find the country's biggest surface water reservoir sitting on top of Harrow Hill. Yet, thanks to Hill Trust pressure following a public enquiry in 1970, the Harrow Park site has been so cleverly landscaped that many newer residents are totally unaware of its whereabouts.

Equally happy was the outcome of the long-running Crown Street redevelopment scheme where, from 1980 on, a private developer, working to tough Local Authority guidelines, replaced many long-derelict ruins and empty sites with cottage-style buildings that closely echo the details of the street's original cottage homes.

Such sympathetic acknowledgement of the past – virtually unheard of just a few decades ago – says much for the town's ever-increasing awareness of its heritage and, thus, for the good work done by the Harrow Heritage Trust set up in 1985 by a former Mayor of Harrow, Peter Pitt.

Possibly the Heritage Trust's greatest success has been its involvement in the restoration of Headstone Manor, the town's most exciting complex of historic buildings where two late medieval barns still flank the entrance to the country's oldest surviving timber-framed and moat-surrounded house.

Although the larger of these barns now houses the highly successful Harrow Museum and Heritage Centre, much restoration has still to be done on all these buildings and it is the Trust's hard-hitting Appeal (fortuitously followed by a National Lottery Grant) that has ensured the work's ultimate completion.

The eighties also saw the equally satisfying regeneration of yet another historic building when the Elliott Hall, the only surviving block of the vast Royal Commercial Travellers' School at Hatch End, was opened as the Harrow Arts Centre in 1988.

Today, under the auspices of the Harrow Arts Council, to which more than 90 arts and cultural groups are affiliated, the Elliott Hall and its adjoining studios provide a varied and highly enterprising programme that goes some way to disguise the fact that the town still lacks a public theatre to call its own.

The entrance to the St. Ann's Centre,
the building that has probably done most to change the look of Central Harrow.

41. A Brief Look at the Nineties

The prospect of a theatre came tantalisingly close in 1994 when Harrow School suggested that the town might wish to make use – at least during the vacations – of the theatre they proposed building to aid the school's drama studies.

Unfortunately, in making this genuinely generous gesture, the Governors failed to anticipate the degree of resistance to their project by many residents of the Hill – and beyond.

From the outset, the school's choice of a site bordering the tranquil Church Fields dismayed many who felt that age-old views could be ruined. Yet such opponents might have been placated were it not for a further disastrous decision to partially finance the scheme by erecting – as a purely commercial venture – a small estate of houses hard by the theatre itself.

If the cat were not already among the pigeons, fur and feathers began to fly in earnest and the normally friendly Hill community was riven with a series of increasingly bitter meetings and demonstrations.

From the ensuing public enquiry, the school emerged the victor and both the theatre – the impressively equipped almost 500-seater Ryan – and the houses duly arose on the chosen site.

By then, of course, there was little question of town and gown sharing the premises since the most vocal of the protesters claimed the result would simply be a year-round, rather than a term-time, nuisance.

Five years on, there is no doubt that the theatre has handsomely proved its value to the school without, it seems, provoking further acrimony. On occasions, such as the annual St. Mary's Music Festival, the building has even been specially licensed for public performances – possibly a pointer to its ultimate role in the 21st century.

The whole controversy was particularly sad in the light of the school's previously excellent record of house-keeping on the Hill, which, in relatively recent times, has permitted eleven boarding houses to be modernised and many impressive new buildings to be erected to almost universal acclaim. One, the handsome central dining room off the High Street, even won a Civic Trust Award.

Admittedly, the new swimming pool and sports complex overlooking the football fields provoked controversy but this could hardly be laid at the door of the school. However, once the decision to sell off the existing open-air pool (the famous "Ducker") had been made, the rules of the Charity Commissioners demanded that the site go to the highest bidders who happened to be the Swaminaryan Hindu Mission.

Their plans to construct what was widely accepted to be the largest Hindu temple outside the Orient again provoked massive protests – and a public enquiry. This time, the result was a victory for the protesters and Ducker, sadly overgrown, still exists, although Ducker Cottage and the Watford Road footbridge that once connected football fields and pool have

Lower Mead, Wealdstone Football Club's popular ground, once occupied the area behind the present Safari cinema.

The same site now houses a busy Tesco superstore.

subsequently been demolished.

As for the town's regular swimmers, many of them were left high and dry when, in 1995, the Harrow Leisure Centre in Christchurch Avenue, Wealdstone, was obliged to close its doors after the discovery of potentially dangerous faults in its electrical wiring and concern about the building's high levels of asbestos.

The fact that the building has been opened only 20 years before – by the sporting Princess Anne – merely added to the general gloom and it seemed a long two years before the Centre reopened in 1997. It had then been almost totally transformed at a cost of some £6 million, of which something over a third came from National Lottery sources.

In mid-decade, another famous building was also obliged to close its doors to the general public. This was the once-celebrated King's Head Hotel on Harrow Hill which, following an unhappy decline in reputation, lost its trading licence. After some years as a refugee hostel, it now seems likely to be sold although the Local Authority – working with the Harrow Hill Trust – has imposed strict guidelines for any potential developer. These envisage the possibility of a superior restaurant or inn within a building that is elsewhere converted into residential accommodation; however, a further suggestion that the Assembly Rooms wing might be demolished for a mews development could yet lead to further heartburn for local residents.

Meanwhile, at the other end of the High Street, the parish church of St. Mary's attained the 900th anniversary of the consecration recorded in Chapter 2. Its foundation by Lanfranc was, of course, a full seven years earlier.

Other Hill institutions proved less long-living, the 1906 Harrow Hospital, as we have read, bidding farewell to its last patients in December 1998. Other familiar buildings retained their names but not their functions, so that visitors to the Hill now find an estate agent at "The Old Fire Station" and a design office at "The Old Bank".

Appropriately enough, on St. George's Day, 1996, Central Harrow gained the vast St. George's Centre, just yards away from the earlier St. Ann's Centre. This time around, the objective was clearly to provide not so much a shopping mall as a recreational complex, complete with bars, restaurants and a 9-screen cinema.

As such, it was welcomed by the town's contemporary Director of Development Services as "a significant factor in maintaining and improving the vitality and viability of Harrow Town Centre".

At first, however, the definition of vitality as made by gangs of youthful rowdies necessitated the installation of stricter security measures but, for the most, the Centre now brings much needed animation to the local scene, especially after dark.

Its dome and spectacular fascia, floodlit in a curiously ghostly green, have also totally changed the views from the Kodak side of town though not everyone would agree that such change is truly an improvement.

Faced with the competition of nine screens in the new complex, the former Granada in Sheepcote Road closed for business after nearly 60 years, subsequently sparking off a sincere if low-key campaign to save a listed building that still houses one of the country's finest

The Elliott Hall at Hatch End survives today as the Harrow Arts Centre.

The historic Headstone Manor Barn has also been brought back to life as the Harrow Museum and Heritage Centre.

surviving Wurlitzer organs. Its near-contemporary, the one-time Dominion, was happily saved by becoming a showcase for Asian movies.

The 1990s also saw Wealdstone Football Club, roughly as old as the century, move out of its Lower Mead ground, off Station Road, to make way for a gigantic Tesco superstore.

To its credit, Wealdstone has managed to keep on playing, sharing grounds with, among others, Watford, Yeading and Edgware. In 1999, the club looks forward to a new home in a custom-built stadium at the Prince Edward Playing Fields in St. David's Drive, Edgware.

For the rest, it was largely a decade of supermarket building with many of the biggest chains adding to their tally of local stores.

Having successfully opened in Harrow Weald, Waitrose – not without controversy – took over the old gas works site in Northolt Road, South Harrow. Safeway, already in North Harrow and Queensbury, achieved a further massive presence alongside the Elliott Hall in Hatch End while Sainsbury's founded big new superstores in Pinner and Kenton as well as a Homebase store in Harrow Weald.

For months, if not years, it seemed likely that Asda would move into Wealdstone. Many thought its presence would help regenerate a shopping area left somewhat stranded by the recent building of a bypass road. Others, equally strongly, declared that Asda's ambitious plans would merely swamp the area, providing the ultimate blow to existing traders.

In the end, the argument became highly political (which this book is not) and Asda found it equally politic to withdraw from the scheme.

Building of Harrow School's Ryan Theatre created much local controversy.

Lively, informal and traffic-free, today's St. Ann's Road is a far cry from the conventional shopping street known to earlier generations.

42. Harrow at Century's End

What, after one thousand years, are we to make of the place which some 210,000 of us now call home?

Since the question is not an easy one – and our answer may well depend on factors such as age and circumstance – a few statistics may prove of help.

For a start, Harrow is not quite so populous as its crowded trains and buses may sometimes suggest. According to the latest figures from the Office of National Statistics (September 1998), there are now 210,900 people resident in the borough – not a huge number if you consider that Harrow's population was already close to 200,000 in 1939.

The true period of growth, as Chapter 35 recalls, was the decade between 1921 and 1931 when the population literally doubled, later reaching a peak of 222,000 in the 1950s.

One other factor is certain sure. Today's population is the most ethnically diverse the town has ever known; indeed, a profile of local ethnic minorities and refugee communities, published as recently as June 1999, shows that over one-third of Harrow's citizens now belong to these groups. This number, moreover, is expected to increase over the next decade.

This new multi-culturalism is, of course, most noticeable in our local LEA Schools where, at the time of writing, just under half the pupils in primary schools (47.2 per cent) and just over half those in secondary schools (55.6 per cent) came from ethnic minorities.

A whole book could – and possibly should – be written about the reasons for and the impact of these changes: suffice to say here that our changing population has vastly enriched many aspects of our community life.

One thinks, in particular, of the arts scene where classical Indian dance or Afro-Caribbean rhythms are now as welcomingly familiar as choruses from Gilbert and Sullivan. Against this background, it comes as no surprise to learn that the 1999 St. Mary's Music Festival drew one of its biggest audiences for a sitar and tabla recital.

The excellence of other cuisines has also brought considerable improvement to our daily menus, whether eating at home or enjoying dishes from around the world in restaurants throughout the borough.

Harrow's traditional churches and chapels are also slowly being joined by monuments to other faiths and, although (as reported in Chapter 29) a vast Hindu temple was not permitted at the foot of Harrow Hill, a Moslem mosque with a dome and minaret, reportedly "as tall as a 12-storey building" will arise in the year 2000 in Station Road just a few doors from where members of the Muslim community have been meeting for the past 14 years.

Given its highly significant siting, virtually opposite our Civic Centre, it may yet serve as a symbol for a new multi-cultural Harrow.

What other statistics concerning our borough deserve to be recorded at century's end?

The recently established University of Westminster now has extensive halls of residence.

The A. A. Headquarters (centre) and the Bernays Institute (right)
show the coexistence of new and old in today's Stanmore Broadway.

Office blocks in Lyon Road epitomise the new "high-rise" Harrow.

Crowds thronging Harrow Leisure Centre after its reopening demonstrate the current popularity of personal fitness.

Like it or not, Harrow's new St. George's Centre is a remarkable piece of modern architecture.

Possibly the fact that, in 1997, some 16 per cent of us were already pensioners although this should be balanced by the knowledge that a healthy (in every sense) 20.9 per cent were under 17.

As for our work force, some 3.4 per cent were then unemployed, compared to the Greater London figure of 6.7 per cent although, it has to be admitted, some 60 per cent were obliged to look outside the borough for their employment. Nevertheless some 4000 businesses now operate in the area, including many nationally-known names such as Kodak (whose Wealdstone plant is still the largest of the company's U.K. operations), GEC Marconi, First National Bank, Ladbrokes and Bovis.

But does Harrow offer much more than a roof (usually a "3-bedroom semi" roof) above our heads?

John Lyon would not be the only one to be surprised by the sheer diversity and, for the most part, excellence of the borough's schools. And how amazed Marion Hewlett would be to realise that her early "technical classes" have blossomed into the Harrow campus of the University of Westminster off the Watford Road, now planning for over 7000 student places by century's end.

As for transport, we have come a long way (though, some might say, not far enough) from the days when Prime Minister Lord Palmerston was obliged to ride to Harrow on his favourite white horse.

At the risk of sounding like an official "Welcome to Harrow" brochure, it should also be added that our town scores remarkably well in more material matters.

Earlier chapters have charted the growth (some would say dominance) of the supermarkets without, in fact, mentioning the equivalent spread of restaurants. In comparison with just a few years ago, when many shopping parades were totally dead and deserted by early evening, most districts now offer the pleasures of "take-away" or "eat-in" well into the night.

As for drinking places, our public houses (some renamed for a younger clientele) and wine bars now threaten to be as ubiquitous as those of the 1870s when Harrow was known to have some 27 inns and 27 beer-houses.

Out of doors, Harrow has gained much from the farsightedness of earlier administrators who fought hard for a workable Green Belt policy. Today, a significant portion of the borough's 19 square miles is open space – parks, commons, woods, recreation grounds and sports fields – all available for public use.

This is a fact of which the borough has long been proud and is currently reflected in its coat of arms on which Hygeia, goddess of Health, and a monk support a shield decorated with trees and a highly symbolic band of green.

To these blessings, for such they are, must be added the incomparable richness of the town's historical associations.

Harrow, in fact, offers the best kind of history, the history in which all can share because it lives on in the countless surviving churches, institutions and houses, great and small, to be found throughout the borough.

So, even if Central Harrow sometimes feels distressingly like Watford or Croydon or any one of a hundred British or European townscapes, we can still draw strength and satisfaction from, say, a walk up Harrow or Stanmore Hill, a stroll down Pinner High Street, a service at St. Mary's, Harrow, or an afternoon ramble over Harrow Weald Common.

Problems, of course, remain. Inevitably, many of them – from crime to traffic delays – are of a sort totally unknown to our ancestors but, at least, there seems a willingness to confront them.

In this context, it can only be hoped that improvements will result from a very new (1998) civic initiative.

Called the Harrow Partnership, it is bringing together virtually all the major organisations in the borough in an attempt to improve our overall quality of life by recognising and addressing the most important issues of the day.

In the ultimate, of course, any response to life in Harrow at the end of the second millennium must, of necessity, be a personal one and perhaps the author should be allowed the final word.

Having been born in Harrow and having lived all his life within its boundaries, he has absolutely no intention of moving out; indeed, it would require all the strength and stamina of those proverbial wild horses even to begin to drag him away.

Bibliography

Sources consulted by the author, which may be recommended for further reading, include the following publications:

A World Apart Daphne Rae
The Airship VC Raymond Laurence Russell
Allegra Armistead Gordon
Allegra Iris Origo
Anglo-Saxon England Professor F.M. Stenton
Annals of My Early Life Charles Wordsworth
Architectural History of Harrow Church Samuel Gardner
Attlee Kenneth Harris
Autobiography Charles Merivale
Autobiography Anthony Trollope
Babington Plot Alan Gordon Smith
The Beeton Story Nancy Spain
Bellamies of Uxendon W. Done Bushell
The Benefactions of John Lyon B.P. Lascelles (printed as a pamphlet 1906)
The Book of Harrow E.D.W. Chaplin
The Book of Wealdstone R.S. Brown
Brasses of Middlesex H.K. Cameron
Byron Frederick Raphael
Church & Community J.H. Bettey
Church Life on Harrow Hill 767–1547 Rev. W. Done Bushell
Collins Guide to Parish Churches
The Country Parish Anthony Russell
The Countryside Lies Sleeping Alan W. Ball
Doomsday Geography of S.E. England (Cambridge University Press 1962)
Drummonds of Charing Cross Hector Bolitho
The English Parish Church Gerald Randell
English Social History G.M. Trevelyan
English Society In The Early Middle Ages Doris Stenton
English Society In The Later Middle Ages Maurice Keen
Environs of London Rev. Daniel Lysons
Extraordinary Popular Delusions Charles MacKay
Fair Enough Jim Golland
First Five Lives of Annie Besant Arthur H. Nethercot
First Four Minutes Roger Bannister
Frederick Goodall R.A. N.G. Sharpe
From Rural Middlesex to London Borough Arthur Dark
Gilbert, His Life & Strife Hesketh Pearson
The Goodliest Place in Middlesex Eileen M. Bowlt
Greenhill Harry Wilkins
Handel, Canons and The Duke of Chandos R.A. Streatfield
The Harrow Apprentices Jim Golland
Harrow in Poetry & Prose Ed. George Townsend Warner
Harrow Life of Henry Montagu Butler Edward Graham
Harrow Public School Life Archibald Fox
Harrow Recollections Sidney Daryl
Harrow School E.D. Laborde
Harrow School Howson/Warner (1898)
Harrow Through The Ages W.W. Druett
History of Christianity Caroline T. Marshall
History of the Church of England Henry Wakeman (1908)
History of the Free School of Harrow Rudolph Ackermann
Horatia Nelson Winifred Gerin
How Old Is That Church? Pamela Cunningham
Illustrated History of Harrow School Lichfield/Shymansky/Golland
Illustrated Notes on English Church History Rev. A.C. Lane (1904)
The Indomitable Mrs Trollope Eileen Bigland
Isabella and Sam Sarah Freeman
Layman's History of the Church of England G.R. Balleine (1913)
Life and Death of Thomas Becket George Greenaway
Life, Letters & Journals of Lord Byron Thomas Moore
Life, Manners and Travels of Fanny Trollope Johanna Johnston
Life of St. Anselm Eadmer Ed. R.W. Southern
Life of St Thomas & Historia Novorum in Anglia The Good Monk Eadmer
London & Birmingham Railway Through Harrow Peter G. Scott
Lordship of Canterbury F.R.H. De Boulay
Middlesex J. Norris Brewer
Middlesex C.W. Radcliffe
Middlesex Michael Robbins
Mr & Mrs Beeton H. Montgomery Hyde
My Early Life Winston S. Churchill
My Life Oswald Mosley
My Line of Life Heath Robinson
Old Harrow Days J. Cotton Minchin
One Hundred Years of Wimbledon Lance Tingay
One Look Back George W. Russell
Oswald Mosley Robert Skidelsky
Oxford Book of Royal Anecdotes Ed. Elizabeth Longford
Oxford History of Britain Ed. Kenneth O. Morgan
Paintings, Prints and Drawings of Harrow Hill Alan W. Ball
The Parish Registers of Harrow On The Hill W.D. Cooper
The Perpetual Curate of Pinner and His Lady Patricia A. Clarke (The Pinn No 4, 1991)
Personal and Professional Recollections Gilbert Scott
Plague, Population and the English Economy John Hatcher
Pinner Patricia A. Clarke
Pinner Through The Ages W.W. Druett
Place Names of Stanmore and District R.W. Thomson
The Pre-Conquest Church In England Margaret Deanesley
Rambles Around Eton and Harrow Alfred Rimmer
Reader's Digest Yesterday's Britain
Recollections of Schooldays At Harrow (1890) Rev. H.J. Torre
The Registers of St. Mary's Vol I & II Ed. W.O. Hewlett
Reminiscences of a Harrow Master C.H.P. Mayo
Reportorium Ecclesiasticon Richard Newcourt
Roxeth Remembered Compiled D.R. Pratt
Saint Anselm Dean Church (1905)
Saints & Scholars David Knowles
Sheridan W.A. Darlington
Signposts To The Past Margaret Gelling
Some Antiquities of Middlesex Sir Montagu Sharpe
Some Notable Archbishops Montague Fowler (1895)
Sometime A Soldier Geoffrey Woolley
Stanmore Past Eileen M. Bowlt
Stanmore Through The Ages W.W. Druett
Story of Roxeth T.L. Bartlett
A Tour Through England and Wales Daniel Defoe
The Wealdstone Scene H.M. Wilkins
Wembley Through The Ages M. Elsley
What I Remember Thomas Trollope
The World of Sir Gilbert Scott David Cole

Other material has been drawn from Records relating to the Parish of Harrow and the Northwick Collection of Documents, currently lodged at the Greater London Records Office. In addition, the unpublished local history researches of Audrey Boardman, Kenneth Glyn Charles, Jennifer Foyle and Agnes Wyatt have been consulted with gratitude together with English Historical Documents, The Victorian County History, Handbook for the Use of Visitors to Harrow on the Hill, George Thomas Clark's Report to the General Board of Health (1849), Papers relating to Harrow and Harrow School, the Antiquarian Researches of the London & Middlesex Archaeological Society, the Survey of Church Livings at the Time of The Commonwealth as well as collected issues of St. Mary's Parish Magazine, Harrow Gazette, Harrow Observer, The Gentleman's Magazine, The Builder, The Ecclesiologist and The Harrovian.

Index